From Patagonia to Professor

Meredith Temple-Smith

From Patagonia to Professor

For Lucho, explorer, friend and naturalist extraordinaire, without whom this trip would not have been possible.

From Patagonia to Professor
ISBN 978 1 76109 563 4
Copyright © text Meredith Temple-Smith 2023
Cover images: Peter Temple-Smith – the author holding the shrunken head

First published 2023 by
GINNINDERRA PRESS
PO Box 3461 Port Adelaide 5015
www.ginninderrapress.com.au

Contents

Prologue	7
South America 1985: The beetle man	15
Getting down to business	22
A gift	30
The spirits in the trees	36
Visiting Lago Chapo	43
To Argentina with contraband	51
Patagonia	56
Looking for the Patagonian opossum	61
Towards the sea	71
Cleaning up	75
Pico Salamanca	80
La Madrugada	87
Mauricio exposed	91
Back to Chile	93
Five become seven	97
More water	101
Glacier	106
Chaiten to Chiloé	109
In one end and out the other	115
Lago Chapo revisited	119
Puyehue 2	124
Goodbye David	128
Puyehue 3	131
Northward bound	135
Departure	141

Australia 2016	145
Reality check 2020	181
For those interested in the fieldwork	185
References	190
Acknowledgements	192

Prologue

I have a photo on the wall of my office. It shows me in profile, thirty years ago, face to face with a genuine shrunken head. Although smiling in the photo, only minutes before when I first saw it, I had been shaking. I had never before seen a shrunken head. I had no idea that the identity of the owner would be so...present. It was impossible not to be affected by the intimacy of holding a stranger's head in my hands. Who was this man? He looked to be in his late fifties or early sixties. He had short white hair, and a white beard stained with what looked like nicotine. He had a bulbous nose on which enlarged pores and broken veins could be clearly seen. His florid colouring suggested he was someone who had been a big drinker. His skin was coarse and mostly rough, and at the back of his neck, where the head had been opened to remove his skull, the skin was rough-cut and felt and looked exactly like leather. I was holding the head of someone who had actually been alive! Before this, I wondered whether shrunken heads were real, but holding this I was certain that sixty to a hundred years ago this man had been alive.

This photo was taken on my very first day in Chile in 1985, at the home of Luis E. Pena Guzman, a well-known entomologist in Chile who was to guide our zoological field trip through Chile and Argentina; the whole trip would include four months in South America followed by three months in London.

Before my husband Peter and I left, we were interviewed by *Woman's Day*, which was 'Australia's brightest weekly', according to its tag line. Although conducted weeks before we left in October 1985, the article came out in February 1986, by which stage we had finished the South American leg and were in London. There were three photos in the

NewsMaker section on page 43, with a brief accompanying article describing them. Curiously, all three of the female news makers depicted in that issue shared the same first name. Meredyth Judd and Harvey Shore were an Australian couple who made news because they had 'A Marriage Made In India', performed at the Taj Mahal. Meredith Allison was a twenty-four-year-old who made news for 'Dealing With Emotions' by being a fifth-generation funeral director. Meredith Taylor (me) made news for 'Roughing It For Science' and the first part of the article stated,

> The possibility that a South American marsupial could be an ancestor of the Australian marsupial is to be explored by Peter Temple-Smith, a reproductive biologist and lecturer in anatomy in Melbourne's Monash University. Peter will try to establish the link by examining the sperm of a marsupial the natives call Monito del Monte, on a trip to South America with his wife, Meredith.

At the time we were interviewed for the article, I was thirty years old and had been married for four years.

Peter and I had met in 1977 at Monash University's halls of residence, where we both had after-hours roles as tutors. Peter had grown up in Tasmania. In those days, he was a tall man with sturdy legs and a lush brown beard. He both loved and was comfortable in the bush. He is enthusiastic about everything outdoors – from home-grown vegetables to the call of the spur-winged plover. His great ability to remember interesting facts and communicate science means he is a fascinating companion. He was, and remains, a great conversationalist and a very charming man.

In contrast to Peter, I had no knowledge and almost no experience of the bush, and truthfully, was scared of the dark. I was impressed by the fact that after Peter finished his PhD he had lived in New York for three years, and that he played guitar and had sung in bands as a student. I thought this sign of his creativity complemented my passion for dance. I used to go to dance classes on campus every day, and definitely at the expense of my studies, I spent most of my days hanging out with other members of the Monash Modern Dance Club, planning or rehearsing performances.

In my final year of study, when I wasn't dancing, I had a part-time job as a research assistant in the Department of Psychology. I was thrilled to be offered this job, which led to the offer of another. Three decades later across a function room I saw the professor who had originally offered me the job. With the confidence of many years of academic work behind me, it occurred to me that I should thank him for nurturing the seeds of my career. I reminded him of who I was, and the experiments I had run for him. I acknowledged that I had not been the best or brightest student in the class, and then I asked if he had seen in me back then some glimmer of academic potential. He gave the matter some thought, and then admitted that he did not recall that I had any aptitude when he offered me the job, it was only that he had a thing for girls with long blonde hair. It's hard to imagine these days that bleached hair was once considered very suggestive, and I was what was disparagingly called a 'bottle-blonde'. Perhaps my professor had been a little hopeful that my personality might live up to the reputation of dyed hair? Whatever the reason, it seems my whole academic career was based on a sham!

In many ways, that story sums up the differences between Peter and me. Peter's curiosity and love of knowledge almost decreed that he would become an academic. My road to academia was accidental, and paved with experiences not entirely of my own making. As a young person I had many dreams but no realistic idea of the direction in which my life might unfold. I loved learning new things and I was, and still am, fascinated by human behaviour. This curiosity may be partly a legacy of having moved homes frequently in my childhood. Being observant about people offered clues about what they liked. I wanted to please people, as it increased the chance of being accepted into their circle.

I had no confidence in my intelligence and was all too aware of the genuine holes in my knowledge. So I was flattered when Peter, seven years my senior and a well-respected junior academic, took an interest in me. When we were married in 1981, I had two goals, neither of which included work. I wanted to have an interesting life, and I wanted to be a mother, goals which were both eventually achieved in unusual ways.

The trip to South America involved four months of data collection in South America, followed by three months at Regent's Park Zoo in London, where Peter was to work with colleagues on related research.

My memory of our arrival in London is still sharp. After months of speaking beginner Spanish, it had been such a relief to arrive somewhere which seemed more like home and where it took no effort to communicate. It was a crisp cold Friday in January 1986, but the sun was shining, the cabbie was friendly and the traffic flowed smoothly as we made our way to Regent's Park Zoo. We felt relaxed and happy to be starting on the second stage of Peter's study leave, particularly given the success of the field trip in Patagonia.

My memory is that we pulled up outside the zoo at the Institute of Zoology near a doorman's booth. We unloaded two suitcases and two carry-ons, as well as a small backpack (his) and a shoulder bag (mine). Peter needed to collect a front door key from his colleague who had offered to put us up until we found accommodation for our three months stay. When we realised the colleague's office was on the first floor, and that there were no lifts, we discussed what to do. I offered to stay with the bags, but Peter really wanted me to go with him to meet his colleague. We decided to leave the bags next to the doorman's booth. The doorman was on the phone, but he seemed to understand our gesticulations and nodded when we indicated we would be back in five minutes.

When we returned fifteen minutes later, my carry-on bag was gone. The doorman said he had seen nothing, and almost seemed not to believe that there had been another bag. He offered to more carefully mind our other luggage while we frantically ran around in every direction that would be open to a traveller on foot, looking for any signs of the theft. When we found a nearby path that led over a small canal our hearts sank, as we realised that anything thrown into that water would be likely lost forever.

We took a cab to the police station to report the loss. While they were somewhat sympathetic about the loss of the beautiful blue lapis lazuli necklace destined for my mother, and my thick and detailed diary in which I had recorded every day of the field trip, it was not until we mentioned the bones that their interest was piqued. We had stored the tiny bones in tissue paper in a cardboard box for safe keeping, which just happened to have the word 'radioactive' printed on it. Actually, it had once contained cards which detected radioactivity, so in reality the box itself was perfectly safe. But perhaps a thief might feel concerned at the potential exposure and hand it in? By this time it was mid-afternoon, and the early winter dusk was falling. With mixed feelings, we took a cab to the house in Golders Green where we were to stay. Although we tried to be optimistic that the bag would be found, already our enthusiasm for this stay in London, so long happily anticipated, had been dampened.

Frustratingly, two days later on the following Monday morning, Peter's colleague told us that the zoo switchboard had taken a call from someone who said they had found some papers with my name on them and some diaries when walking their dog in Primrose Hill. (I pictured a large green hill, dotted with trees circled by primroses, and the eager dog owner following a trail of paperwork to the box with the bones.) When we heard this news, we were so excited, but our hopes were quickly dashed when we heard that the switchboard operator who took the call did not know we had arrived in London yet and suggested the caller call back in a few days. Despite our daily anxious queries, there were no more calls.

We contacted the local newspaper, hoping an article might prompt either the caller to return the papers, or the thief to return the bones. But the thief was unconcerned or illiterate. Despite an article with a scary headline about the box marked 'radioactive' imploring the thief to seek health information, the bones remained missing.

When all of this took place in 1986, there were no mobile phones, and no personal computers, and to have a social network meant something completely different. I have spent many nights awake, wondering whether someone might remember something about this incident that occurred over thirty years ago. The doorman, the thief, the dog-walker, the switchboard operator…could any of them now could help locate the diaries or the bones?

When I wrote the diaries, I imagined reading and rereading them throughout my life to remind me of all of the details of that momentous journey. Even more importantly, I remember that I wrote all kinds of observations about myself. In the intervening years, there have been so many events, the raising of three amazing children, the completion of a DHSc, several job moves, an eventually amicable divorce, the deaths of my parents, the editing and/or writing of five books, and holidays, friends, disasters, pleasures; the stuff of everyday life. Now, with some of my life's achievements behind me, I find myself thinking often of the trip. I long to know whether it provides any clues to explain the surprising path in life I appear to have chosen, or which chose me. I long to read what I wrote in 1985, to see if there are glimmers of the me of today.

So I called Peter and asked him if he could remember whether we ever kept a copy of the police record or the article in the paper. (Even if he did, it could be a quest to locate it. Being academics, we both have houses completely full of books and papers, and it is a miracle we can find anything!)

However, he did lay his hands on three important items: his diary of a field trip in South America that he undertook with close friend and colleague Dr Tom Grant in September 1983, some of which covered places we visited in 1985; an exercise book of field notes, including many in my handwriting, which recorded details of animals which we kept for a little while, their measurements and weights, and observations of their behaviour while they were in captivity; and his trapping notes, which recorded the details of every animal trapped, most of which were immediately released, once identified.

I also found a piece of paper folded inside this book, which was the start of an article I had written. So many pictures come flooding back. I grasp them tightly and start to piece together the story of my travel…

South America 1985
The beetle man

Luis, affectionately known as Lucho, was a famous entomologist with a special interest in coleoptera – the study of beetles – and he contributed many thousands of beetle and other insect samples to natural history museums around the world. He had discovered many new species throughout South America. When not studying and collecting insects in the wild, Lucho lived and worked in a compound of several houses owned by relatives and co-workers at La Cantera, just north of Santiago. His open-plan house was on the top of a hill, and was made of wood and concrete – architect-designed – to ensure plenty of space for his collections of insects and the many artefacts from his trips. The shrunken head I held on my first day in Chile was one of two owned by Lucho. The other was that of a young girl, maybe twelve or thirteen years of age, with long black hair and colouring suggestive of Amazonian Indian origin.

Lucho had once had a traditional academic position at a university, but he loved fieldwork too much to be trapped inside a lecture theatre. He often assisted international scientists to travel in Chile and other countries in South America, by being the guide and provisioner for their field trips. He was planning to use our trip to collect beetles and butterflies, while Peter and I set traps to catch a tiny marsupial affectionately called the little monkey of the forest – *monito del monte* – to test a theory Peter had about the origin of Australian marsupials. We were also going to search for *Lestodelphys halli*, the Patagonian opossum. The only previous evidence of this species had been five individuals caught by the naturalist Budin in 1935. Peter hoped to find more living specimens and record more of their biology.

Lucho had apparently been hesitant and unenthusiastic when he learnt that I was to accompany Peter on the field trip. This made me feel very uncomfortable when I found out after I arrived in Santiago. When Peter told me, I resolved to prove to Lucho that his fears of taking me were unfounded. He later told me that he had only once or twice taken women on field trips, and he had not found it an easy experience. Once we had left civilisation far behind, the reasons for this became very clear, as the fieldwork took precedence over everything else, including basic hygiene, as you will see. Lucho said on the one occasion he took a woman and a baby on an overnight fieldwork trip he was horrified to find that the woman changed the baby's nappy *inside* the van! That comment encapsulated Lucho's eccentricity and level of dedication to his work, as hundreds of insects, dead and alive, alongside cyanide and other chemicals, covered all the food preparation surfaces inside the van, including at mealtimes.

I was very excited to go on the field trip, and although I loved the idea of being intrepid, I was not at all brave and had had very little experience even of camping. Peter, in contrast, had had a childhood in Tasmania which sounded like it was set in a *Boy's Own Annual* from the 1950s: getting up early and leaving his parents a note saying 'Gone fishing'; rowing out to rocky outcrops to observe birds; climbing mountains; swimming on beaches with no lifeguards. I was the kind of child who ran away from shallow waves as they came into shore. My only childhood experience with walking through the bush was going between road and sea to access Melbourne's beaches in the summer, and wending my way through patches of bush soon destined to make way for housing developments near where we lived. After Peter and I got together in the 1970s, I had more exposure to camping. But there were some things I still found challenging. He preferred not to use lanterns or torches but to allow his own vision to adjust to the dark. I hated the dark. I especially disliked having to go outside the tent a night and dig a toilet hole, do your business and then cover it up. But I accepted that being married to a zoologist would mean that I either needed to have long periods of time without him while he was in the field, or else I would need to find aspects of fieldwork rewarding in some way so that we could spend time together. In the *Women's Weekly* article 'Roughing It For Science', the paragraph briefly describing our quest finishes with the words

> In a land where women are kept in the background, Meredith, who has been learning Spanish, will dress like a man and cover her blonde hair with a scarf. She will also undertake her own project, studying animal behaviour.

Of course I don't recall actually saying anything to the reporter about my planned wardrobe. My past experience of dressing like a man on an Australian field trip had not gone well. Following a weekend at Braidwood in New South Wales, camped by the river trapping platypus, we headed home. I had very short hair and was dressed in woollen khaki army surplus trousers, stout leather boots, and a blue checked woollen shirt; perfect for protecting the skin from insects and scratches when walking through the bush. On the way home, we stopped at a small town to use the public toilets. As I was walking into the ladies' facilities, I noticed several older women reboarding a nearby bus. Once inside, I had to wait for a free toilet. When an old lady eventually emerged from the cubicle she said, "You're in the wrong toilet, sonny!' I tried to remonstrate but when I did, she hit me several times with her handbag. I ran outside. When I told Peter what had happened, he laughed and put his arms around me, undoubtedly further horrifying any other short-sighted bus passengers, as public interactions between same-sex couples were rare in those days. While my short haircut may have contributed on that occasion to a mistaken identity, I am quite sure that covering my, by this stage, shoulder-length bleached hair with a scarf would not fool any South Americans even with poor eyesight!

However, the reporter was right in saying I planned to undertake a project of my own on animal behaviour. This was the story Peter told to Lucho to ensure that he would not refuse to take me on the field trip. In fact, I knew that if I did not get involved in some aspect of fieldwork, there would be little for me to do during the four months we planned to be pretty much out in the middle of nowhere. I thought I could assist Peter by noting all the details of the trip that might be relevant to the fieldwork, including but not limited to animal behaviour, because for me humans are the most interesting animals of all. What else could I do? Space for personal possessions was very limited, and I could take only a single novel. I had spent ages before we left, seeking advice on which novel to take. Would it be a favourite that I could re-read? Or should it be a challenging book? In the end, on the advice a work colleague (thanks, David), I took William Thackeray's *Vanity Fair*. I would ration myself to read no more than a few pages a day, which was to be my reward for recording the daily events of the trip.

Before we left Santiago, we went shopping for supplies. I remember noticing the contrasts between Santiago and Buenos Aires, from where we had recently arrived. Buenos Aires had a European feel to it – large, gracious old buildings, often in great need of repair, and wide streets. I didn't feel we stood out in any way from the locals. But the Santiago of 1985 was different. Everyone, at least in the areas we visited for our shopping on that day, looked much shorter than me, with darker skin and darker hair. There were more people on foot, and the buildings and the people looked poorer. That was the very first time I ever saw children selling small items of food to people in cars when they stopped at the lights. When the lights turned green, it was nerve-racking watching the young sellers dash between the cars as the traffic surged forward.

In the heart of Santiago, I went to several stores, trying to find exactly the right kind of book in which to record the details of the trip. I had absolute faith in my husband. I was convinced that the trip would be a success. I also knew that this whole experience would be new and vastly different from my previous life. I wanted to be sure that any interesting observations, of which I imagined there would be many, weren't recorded on scraps of paper. Clearly, I had invested a lot of hope in the diary even before I began to write it!

Eventually, we found a large stationery store with aisles festooned with boxes and overflowing shelves which suggested possibilities galore. I joyfully made my selection, but became slightly confused by the purchasing process. Eventually, I was guided through. I went to one counter to pay, and my purchase was taken to another counter for wrapping in waxy brown paper. I was given a handwritten slip to take to the cashier, who sealed my money into a container and posted it into a transparent pneumatic tube transporter. The container with my money went upstairs to a glass-walled office, where the money was removed by a serious bespectacled man. He placed my change back inside the container, which was sucked back to the cashier's desk. Once I received the change and a new slip, I was able to exchange the slip for my goods at the wrapping counter. The process had taken about fifteen minutes, and involved four staff members of different ages, all with expressions which reflected the serious responsibilities of this level of teamwork.

Smaller in size than an Australian exercise book, my choice for my diary was a thick lined book with a shiny bright blue cover. The word AUCA was on the cover, with the tiny letters M R beneath it and the number sixteen over the number twenty, next to it. The red and white geometric pattern down the right-hand side took up less than a quarter of the cover. I bought three of the books, and used one as a flower press. I still have that book, containing many unidentified and now desiccated floral remnants. In one of the other books, I began my diary. On the first page, I remember I wrote the names of the five of us travelling on the field trip, with our country of origin underneath the name. In a letter I subsequently wrote to my parents, I stated that

> I am keeping a diary – fairly detailed, although I may not be able to keep it up. So far, I have written eighty pages in ten days. It's very tiring, and of course once you have written it all down once, you lose the desire to rewrite it as part of a letter – so Peter will have to contribute either to the letters or the diary. He's here beside me dissecting a dead rat and two lizards. He'll have to move away soon as we are about to have lunch – potatoes in white sauce and bread. I'll try to imagine it is a French salad with some very lemony dressing.

I remember as I wrote those words that I felt a small thrill about the adventure I was on. I had already imagined a million different scenarios around our trip, some good and some terrifying. I had imagined one or both of us getting injured or sick. I had imagined falling off a cliff, being caught in a landslide, being kidnapped. My way of coping with anxiety was to imagine every possible negative outcome, on the assumption that I would be unlikely to accurately predict the eventual outcome. I very deliberately wouldn't imagine any good outcomes, thereby ensuring that a good outcome would eventuate. This had been a long-held, if ridiculous, strategy that stemmed from childhood. As a child, I had a vivid imagination, evident in some of my primary school exercise books which I still have. When I was in my fourth year of school, I wrote a story called 'Snake', which now seems an uncanny foretelling of some of my life. It is reproduced here with the original spelling, punctuation, and continuity errors.

Canoeing down the Orange River seemed great fun to the twins, James and Jane. But for Mother it was a worry. Why, there were snakes and wild animals that could hurt them! Mr. Thompson was a botanist and had come with his family to Africa to study wild flowers. He had been asked to go canoeing down the Orange River to find a new sort of Ivy.

The day of departure came. With two large canoes packed with rugs, tents, pots, food and water, there was scarcely room for them to fit. At sunset they pulled into shor set up the tents and made a campfire. The children were sent to bed and Mr. and Mrs. Thompson stayed up to drink mugs of hot coffee.

Suddenly they heard a scream! Following the sound they came to Jane, crying out for them to kill the snake. Beside her lay two dead snakes and a third one over near a bush. She had been bitten three times. Mr. Thompson carried Jane back to camp where Mrs. Thompson gave her First Aid. Her father paddled her to the Natives Hostpital where she was given proper treatment. When she felt better her father said,

'Jane, why did you go out of the tent, we told you not to.'

'Daddy, I lost the gold watch you lent me and I was so afraid you would get in a rage and go mad at me,' said Jane timidly.

'Why did you call out for me to kill the snake, – there was three dead already.'

'There was a whole family of them. They came after me. Oh! Yes, I remember, someone came out of the jungle I don't know who he was, – he killed three of the snakes and four of them went wriggling in your direction.

'Jane, was this person a native?'

'Yes, I think so.'"

When Mr. Thompson arrived at the camp he went to the spot where he found Jane. Sure enough, there was a small boy about 6 hiding in the jungle. He took the child with him back to the camp. The boy, whose name was Wabna, was an orpahn who had been wandering around searching for food when he heard Jane's scream. He ran and killed three of the snakes and was frightened when Mr. Thompson came so he jumped back into the jungle.

A few weeks later Jane was back to normal. Before they left, Mr. Thompson said to Wabna, 'Would you like to stay with us? My wife and I would like to adopt you and the children would too.'

Wabna did want to and they finished their trip in happiness.

This composition, as essays seemed to have been called then, was marked 8½, with the comment 'Good'. Even though I like to see this early evidence of my imaginative writing, I also cringe at the evidence of my white, colonial, patriarchal presumptions.

The story reminds me that, unlike the rest of my family, I was fascinated by the natural world. At school, we studied spiders, and around the time I wrote this composition I must have expressed my interest, as for my next birthday my parents bought me a child's microscope. I spent hours examining bits of insects and leaves. I had absolutely no idea of what I was looking at, but I liked the idea of being able to see things that other people couldn't. I used to tell people I wanted to be a pathologist when I grew up, to solve the mystery of disease by unlocking the secrets of cells. It seems I always had a passion for a quest.

Getting down to business

We headed off from Lucho's home near Colina, in October 1985, to travel the thousand kilometres south to the first trapping site. We travelled in two vehicles which each seated two people next to the driver – a white station wagon known in Spanish as a *camionetta*, and a large grey campervan, which had a table and seats for four, a sink and an oven, and a bed which fitted two at a pinch, high above the driving cabin. I had been told that Peter and I could sleep in the back of the *camionetta*, and the other three would sleep in the van. This seemed quite civilised and as we left I felt optimistic about the arrangements.

We had huge amounts of equipment, such as a camp stove, tents, ground sheets and tarpaulins, ropes, machetes, a hatchet and a spade. We had everything necessary to perform small operations on live animals, such as scalpels and blades, scissors, disposable gloves, saline and anaesthetic, as well as laboratory supplies needed for preserving animal tissue such as fixative, different-sized plastic beakers and specimen jars, syringes, vials, microscope slides, a cork board and a microscope. We had wet weather gear, head torches and batteries, rubbish bags, compasses, Swiss army knives, and a first aid box. Once all of this and our very limited personal items were stowed away, there didn't seem to be much room, but Lucho had stocked the vehicles with as many tins and other food items as he could, and told us that we would be able to get fresh meat and vegetables as we travelled. Fortunately, I could not foresee what this meant in reality.

Lucho had never married. He was dedicated to his work, and perhaps because it made it easier travelling and camping in the field for weeks, he seemed to employ only younger male assistants. Lucho was a not unattractive man who was then in his late sixties. Both his body and his clothes had the crumpled and slightly monochrome look of someone for whom personal appearance was of less interest. This was evident on the first occasion on which we shared a salad lunch with Lucho. Before that time, I had had no idea that beetroot could act as well as a plaque-disclosing tablet to demonstrate where better efforts are needed in dental care. It was a good lesson and showed me that I should try to sit next to him rather than opposite him at mealtimes, particularly when brightly coloured food was served.

As well as Lucho, there was Checho, Lucho's long-standing assistant, who with his wife and two young children lived in their own house on Lucho's compound at La Cantera. Then there was Pedro, a very young man who had only been working with Lucho for a short time. Neither of these men spoke English, so we needed to use our novice Spanish to communicate with them. Unlike their employer, they both had beautiful white teeth and very clean dark and shiny hair.

The day we set off was warm and sunny and I remember our excitement as we drove down the hill at La Cantera. Checho drove the van, I sat in the middle, trying to ensure my thigh was out of the way of the four-on-the-floor gearstick, and Peter sat beside me. There was Bolivian folk music playing as we drove, and I felt like I was part of something really important.

We were heading south. For the first three hundred kilometres, the weather was mild as we passed through countryside and small townships. We stopped to eat at a café and I remember being thrilled by the freshness and flavour of the salad vegetables; avocado, tomato, lettuce and lemon. If this is what we were to eat, we would go home healthy! But before we left, I went out the back to use the bathroom and was directed to a roofless concrete slab with wooden walls which went from knee to shoulder height. Used toilet paper littered the splashed floor all about the hole in the ground, with a concentration in the corner where the blowflies were having a party at the overflowing and lidless bin. The odour and difficulty in negotiating the use of the hole in the ground pretty much dampened the enthusiasm which had been generated by lunch. Little did I know that bathrooms, or the lack of them, would be a pretty big issue which I would need to face several times a day for the next few months.

The further south we travelled, the colder and more overcast the weather became. The first night we spent in the pouring rain, parked in a petrol station. The roof of the back of the *camionetta* leaked, our sleeping bags became damp very quickly and it was very stuffy. Peter snored and I couldn't sleep with his noise and the airlessness. I woke him up and eventually we both got up and sat in the petrol station's all-night snack bar having coffee. I tried to make light of it, but I was a little shocked at my inability to manage to sleep in the back of the car. It was only the first night; surely there would be many worse sleeping arrangements to come! I shared my doubts and Peter quickly reassured me that all would be well when we arrived the next day at the national park.

Puyehue National Park is situated in the lakes district in the south of Chile, eighty kilometres from the town of Osorno. The road to the park passed by fertile farms with lush green fields and fat cows and sheep standing motionless in the drizzle. Breaks in the swirling mist revealed distant vistas of enormous oaks, elms, poplars and silver birch framed by snow-capped mountains. In contrast to their urban relatives whose houses seemed surrounded only by bare earth, here many Indians lived in small wooden homes in pocket-handkerchief-sized farms which were beautifully tended. Almost all had tiny English gardens with forget-me-nots (in Spanish, *no me olvidas*), climbing roses, irises, Californian poppies, carnations, pansies and jasmine.

There were many Australian gumtrees and wattle trees to be seen as we drove along. My favourite plants were the very attractive native fuchsias which grew as big as large trees, especially near rocks and on banks at the water's edge. We saw people ploughing sodden fields by hand and driving oxen-drawn carts through mud. The caballeros or horsemen wore homespun woollen ponchos, scarves and little felt schoolgirl shaped hats while they worked; the greasy wool was excellent at deflecting the cold and rain.

The foothills of the Andes are in a cold-climate rainy area, where there is no dry season, so everywhere there is evergreen southern beech forest with immensely tall trees and an understorey of shrubs, moss, dead leaves and solid bamboo creepers. The many clear cold streams tumbling over fallen rocks, the dampness underfoot, the climbing vines and red flowers of the native fuchsias were reminiscent of the fairy dells of my childhood imagination.

We arrived on 18 October 1985 at our first campsite, at Termas, Puyehue National Park, where we were all to sleep in an A-frame cabin. Having been told by Lucho that the conditions were excellent, I clearly remember my disappointment once inside the dusty hut. I was so disgusted by the rusty bath and shower curtain with mildew that I remember considering whether to shower at all. In the end, knowing it might be the last opportunity for some months to wash all over, I showered in thongs and took care not to let my body come in contact with the bath or the shower curtain. When we returned to Puyehue to stay for a short time three months later, the story was very different. We had been camping the whole time, and apart from washing in a basin of warm water, the only opportunity to bathe had been a quick run in and out of an icy, fast-flowing stream. I recall that I filled up the bath to the brim and lay in there soaking, lazily observing the attractive colour of the mould, grateful for the warm water and the chance to be completely clean again.

We had arrived late on the Friday night. Peter and I were allocated the privacy of the only bedroom, and the others slept in sleeping bags, on mattresses on iron bedsteads pushed against the walls of the main living area. As I settled down on the old rusty bed with its cold and lumpy mattress, I reflected that it might only have been marginally more comfortable than the night before in the back of the *camionetta*. I was so exhausted that I fell asleep quickly, but I awoke cold and stiff a couple of hours later to the pitch blackness. I lay awake for ages, trying to will myself to ignore my bursting bladder, knowing that to go the toilet would require me to stand up in the freezing air, negotiate my way to the door through to the living area and then to walk in the blackness through to the bathroom. Eventually, I had to go. Even though I closed the door to the toilet, I was aware of how loud the stream of urine sounded as it splashed into the toilet bowl. And then, even worse, the flushing sound and endless filling of the ancient cistern was followed by the creaking and groaning of the pipes as they transported the rusty water to the cistern. Afterwards, I lay in bed, awake for ages, wondering if the men in the living room and the man beside me were already regretting that I was on this trip. I was also wondering if I had bitten off more than I could chew.

Saturday was our first day of laying traps. That morning, we had been very busy making bait for the traps we were about to lay in the evening. Bait needs to be a good texture so that it can be easily rolled into balls; it needs to smell delicious to attract an animal. Often, some traps will be left unbaited, in case an animal finds the bait repugnant but the trap interesting enough to enter. Peter used a standard Australian bait mixture of honey, oatmeal and peanut butter. The bait was rolled into small balls, each wrapped in a piece of gauze to prevent rapid intake by trapped animals, and also to reduce the likelihood of the bait dissolving in the damp conditions. We had a hundred and ten traps which needed new bait almost daily, so making the bait was a large-scale operation which took up almost all the crockery in the hut.

The trapping notes state that Peter, Checho and I set the traps late in the afternoon, at dusk. We laid a hundred Elliot traps and ten 'Tomahawk' wire cage traps in four separate traplines. The Elliot traps looked rather like a large milk carton made of aluminium, which could be flattened for ease of transport. Once opened up and laid on its side, the door at one end is propped up. Bait is placed at the other end, and when an animal enters and walks over a treadle to find the bait, the door snaps shut behind it. The cage traps have a similar mechanism, but are five times the size and the wide gaps in the mesh allow the animal inside to be clearly seen before one sets it free. With the Elliott traps, inserting one's hand to extract the animal within caused me the same level of apprehension as a lucky dip which contained live piranhas! Nowadays, apparently, it is common to upend the trap to allow the animal within to fall into a calico or plastic bag.

Zoologists often lay traps in traplines. The traplines can follow lines on a grid which is superimposed on a map of the area. Recording the number and type of animals found in different seasons in the same area offers some indication of the types and numbers of the local animal inhabitants. The trapping notes detail the four traplines, and state that no grid was used because of the difficulty of the terrain. The first line began ten metres in from the track at a large trunk on an uphill trajectory and extended onto a flatter region and then down to a gully where it was very wet. Each trap was marked by an orange plastic tie, also known as a flagging tape, which was placed at shoulder height above the ground to indicate that there was a trap below, often hidden from sight. Baits were used in all of these traps. Baits were also used in two other traplines, but not in the fourth.

Moving through the bush was not easy, and we were each armed with a machete. Being not very brave by nature, I was relieved to be able to hear the others as they slashed and crashed their way through the forest, even if I could not see them. It took the three of us three and a half hours to lay the traps, as each of the Elliots was inserted into a plastic freezer bag, to offer some protection from the wet to a trapped animal. For this reason, the traps were also laid beneath fallen tree trunks in thickets which might offer some protection if it poured with rain. Usually, some insulating material such as dry leaves or cotton wool is inserted into the traps to prevent the trapped animals from lying on the cold aluminium. Leaf litter, which was often used in Australia in these traps, was too wet in this forest, and I cannot now recall what we used instead.

Mostly, zoologists will check traps during the night, but the trapping notes state that on that first night we did not go out again. Whether that was because it was pouring with rain and very cold (less than five degrees Celsius) is not stated. At eight a.m. on Sunday, we checked the traps, while rain and cold continued unabated. We found six animals. Two male long-haired mice were found in Elliott traps, which probably offered better protection from the elements. A male olive grass mouse was found in a wire cage set underneath a log on the ground. To my horror, one immature female olive grass mouse was found dead in a wire cage, beside a log in the gully. While there are several possible explanations for her death, the possibility that the cold and wet had killed her played on my mind. I wondered if we had checked the traps even thirty minutes earlier she might have survived. I imagined the mouse's mother watching out for the return of her adolescent daughter. Of course at that time I had no real knowledge of mice behaviour, and I have subsequently become aware that once past dependency on adult feeding, many animals cease to interact with their offspring. But at the time, the death of that mouse made a lasting impression on me. My first thoughts were that when I was helping out I would have to step up and not delay the others when coming out to check the traps. Then I suddenly realised that Checho would not always be available; he would sometimes be needed by Lucho. So Peter would actually really need me to help him, regardless of how cold and tired I might be. The enormousness of this task suddenly sank in.

Peter examined the gut contents of the dead female, dissected her skull and dried her skin. The species of the other animals caught in the traps were identified, and they were measured (head size, tail length, anus-genital tubercle, tubercle length), sexed, and marked using a toenail clipping system. This system is temporary, since the nails grow back, and painless for the animal. While he was doing this, the trap lines were checked again that day at five p.m. by Checho and me, and then Peter and I went out again at eleven p.m. to check them. There were no animals either time, but the weather was very cold, raining, and the undergrowth very wet. I remember the acute discomfort of having to put on wet clothes which had not dried out as we headed out each time in the dark, with only a head and hand torch to guide us through the driving rain.

Subsequently we checked the traps each day at five p.m., eleven p.m.

and eight a.m. The number of animals we caught each night varied. To my surprise, quite often we recaptured animals, which we could identify by the common clipped toenail. Recaptured animals were not re-measured, although the recapture site was recorded. Over the first nine days, sixty-four animals – all mice – were caught. That represented a lot of identification of species and of weighing and measuring animals. It also represented a lot of the putting back on of wet clothes and boots to struggle out into the rain. Each morning, we would re-bait and carefully release the animals captured the night before, back to near where they had been caught. The night-time trap checks were often worse – as the wet and the dark compounded the difficulties of making our way through the forest. On a positive note, I was not as frightened of the dark as I had been at the start. I now recognised that the many noises in the forest were only made by small animals, the brothers and sisters of whom I had probably been handling during the day. The one thing I never got acclimatised to, however, was putting on cold wet clothes and struggling through the thick wet undergrowth. After coming in from checking the traps, we would change into dry clothes. But inside the cold hut, the wet clothes never dried, and given our limited clothing we had no choice but to put the wet clothing back on a few hours later. Once back outside in the rain and if walking quickly in the daylight, it didn't seem so bad, but in the icy night air, especially with a wind, that wet clothing was torture.

Those first few days were such a steep learning curve. I had previously been on short field trips with Peter and Tom, his close colleague and friend, often to trap platypusses. But in Australia, even if the trapping was challenging, the customs, language and food were familiar. There was also the feeling that if it all became too cold or stressful, or we were missing some piece of equipment, we could just go home.

But here, in Chile, everything was different and difficult – the weather and terrain were challenging, the animals and the people were new to me and I wasn't really sure how I should behave. I was perpetually tired, physically and emotionally.

A gift

A constant battle for me on this trip was the cold. In a letter home, I wrote,

> I am sitting inside the little hut in which we are staying. I am wearing three pairs of thick woollen socks, woollen trousers (army disposal khaki), a T-shirt, a woollen shirt, woollen jumper and a down jacket, and I am frozen solid, and have been all day. There is no heating in the hut, but there is a gas oven, so we have that on all the time with the door open. Of course, I am constantly worried that the flame will blow out and we will be gassed quietly in our sleep. At night I go to bed fully dressed into my sleeping bag, and I have a blanket on top, and I am still cold. I cannot imagine how the Indians lived here in ancient times wearing only animal skins. My genes would never have survived!

Despite the cold, we were becoming a cohesive little group. Peter directed the work, and I was his right hand. Checho helped when he had no commitments for Lucho. Lucho was also collecting insects, mostly beetles, on this trip, and Pedro assisted him when possible. Lucho and Pedro did most of the cooking or meal preparation.

I could never decide whether the meals were odd because they were prepared by Chileans or prepared by men. However, I suspect the latter. One evening before we left Santiago, Lucho had served us raw clams in their shells. When we squeezed lemon juice on them, they moved. I tried one and when Lucho saw my face, he kindly suggested we put the rest in the oven. And I had thought the grilled cow's udder we tried in a Buenos Aires restaurant was challenging! At least it was dead but it was also nauseatingly thick, spongy and slightly sweet.

The food on the trip was incredibly stodgy and monotonous. Frequently for *desayuno* (breakfast) we had cold porridge, made the night before with tinned condensed milk, sometimes with a slice of fresh apple. For lunch, we had *queso fresco* (fresh cow's cheese), bread, plain sweet biscuits and honey, or else cold porridge with no milk, and bread with condensed milk. I wrote home that while pleasant enough, the lack of variation and constant sweetness left me craving for an orange or a tomato or even a piece of lettuce. Breakfast was around nine thirty or ten a.m. Lunch was around two thirty to three p.m.

The main meal was in the evening, around nine thirty or ten p.m. It mostly comprised rice, potatoes and some kind of protein such as scrambled egg, or tuna in white sauce and, on the odd occasion, meat. It was always followed by bread and honey, and usually for *postres*, or dessert, there would be a slice of quince paste. Occasionally, there was a treat, like a small bar of chocolate, which Lucho divided into five equal parts with surgical precision. As a chocaholic, initially I found this very frustrating, but I have ever since been grateful for this lesson in mindfulness, which taught me the value of slowly savouring each molecule of sweetness.

Despite having no refrigerator, there seemed to be an assumption that all food would keep well in the incredibly cold hut. But I found it repugnant to see fresh meat sitting on a bench for two or three days, uncovered, within a few centimeters of animals in cages, whose droppings were brushed out onto the same bench before being swept up. The differences in my views of safety in food storage were challenged by Lucho on many occasions. The first was when three weeks into our trip, after having noticed the lack of protein in our diet, Lucho proudly produced some bacon brought from Santiago which he had stored all this time in the broken oven in the camper van. It was stilled wrapped in the white butcher's paper, and when he unwrapped it, the fat was moist and the meat was green at the edges. He gleefully put it on a plate to eat, and offered it around. To his surprise, neither Peter nor I took any, and when I commented on his eating it raw, he said that bacon was cured and did not require refrigeration nor cooking! I dare say we are too fussy these days, but nothing would induce me to eat that! What's more, if Lucho suffered any aftermath, he did not let on.

With no TV and very little light to read by in the cabin, our evenings, in between checking the traps, were mostly spent quietly working and talking. Initially, the conversation was mostly focused on the work, and given that Peter, and especially I, were still novice Spanish speakers, it often took a great deal of time to communicate relatively simple messages. The first week or two, we were still learning not only about each other's ability to speak and comprehend, but also about the level of acceptability of different topics of conversation. We also discovered through trial and error that some English phrases cannot be directly translated into Spanish. After much laughing and acting out as I tried to explain the saying 'Any port in a storm', we eventually worked out that the Spanish equivalent was 'Any mule can cross a river.' The English 'Kill two birds with one stone' was almost identical in Spanish as 'Kill two birds with one throw.' However, the very common Australian phrase 'getting caught with your pants down' initially caused disbelief, then hilarity, as the meaning became clear to the Spanish speakers. The Spanish equivalent, apparently, would be translated as 'getting caught with your hands in the dough'. To finally be able to share a laugh with the group was wonderful, and made me feel optimistic about improving my Spanish vocabulary.

Eventually one night, Lucho asked me about my interests, and when I told him that my research interest was sexually transmissible infections, he switched to English to make sure, he said, that he had understood what I said. Then he told me the following tale, which he claimed was completely true. When I said I would love to include it in my diary which might one day be a book, he said that was fine, but to make sure I never revealed the identity of the protagonist.

As I said earlier, Lucho had many young men working for him over the years. He needed assistants with a keen interest in nature and the ability to stay away from home for weeks on field trips with minimal comforts. During those long field trips where interactions with other people are very few and far between, there is plenty of opportunity to talk about life, and to share worries and seek advice. During one field trip, Lucho's assistant, Yaco, told Lucho that his mother was really worried about one of his fourteen younger brothers. This brother, Pichi, was twenty-two, was dissatisfied with life in the village in which they had grown up, and had not yet found a regular job. He had no money, no prospects, and seemed to want to always spend time in town where he was hanging around, she thought, with unsuitable people. His mother despaired for his future and had asked Yaco to try to find him some employment. Yaco asked Lucho whether he could bring Pichi on a field trip next time to see if he liked and could do the work. Lucho agreed, although privately he was pretty certain that the bright lights of the city would prove to be a greater lure to Pichi than hunting for beetles in the forest.

After they returned from their field trip, Yaco went to see Pichi to tell him about he opportunity for undertaking fieldwork on the next expedition, but instead of bringing Lucho news of Pichi's reaction to the offer of work, Yaco rushed back needing urgent medical advice from Lucho. Pichi had slept with a woman in town and he had a terrible itch all around his penis and scrotum. Now he noticed white dots on his pubic hair and was worried his pubic hair was turning white. He couldn't sleep for scratching. In a small house where all the residents slept in a single room, he also feared his mother and siblings could hear him tossing and turning. It was only a matter of time before someone started to ask uncomfortable questions.

Almost immediately, Lucho guessed that Pichi had acquired a case of pubic lice. He explained to Yaco that Pichi would need to go to a doctor to get confirmation of this, and to be checked for other sexually transmissible infections, and then would likely need to purchase treatment from the pharmacy. Both actions would require money and travel to town, as the facilities were not available in a village with only six houses. But Pichi had no money, and was almost beside himself with fear that his mother would discover he had slept with the woman.

So Lucho came up with a clever solution to manage both the infection and the money situation. As an entomologist of reknown in South America, he frequently received requests from museums around the world seeking specimens of insects, preserved in alcohol and mounted on slides for display. They paid quite handsomely for the specimens. Only the preceding week, Lucho had received a request list from the Smithsonian Museum for literally hundreds of specimens, including lice. He suggested his plan to Yaco, who brought a reluctant but relieved Pichi to Lucho's home. There Pichi undressed and lay naked and cold on the kitchen table under a bright light while Lucho and Yaco inspected the situation.

Pthirus pubis are often called crabs because they have a crablike appearance. They are smaller and move more slowly than the head louse, *Pediculus capitis* or the body louse, *Pediculus humanus*. Across the globe, pubic lice feed on the blood of humans. Usually, they infest the pubic hair or hair around the anus but occasionally can be found wherever hair is sparse and coarse. Pubic lice are grey in colour with a small head, a broad oval body, and six legs with claws, four of which are huge compared with the first pair. The claws allow the louse to grasp the hair, while it pierces the skin and sucks with its mouth parts, ingesting blood intermittently over several hours. At each puncture site, a red swelling develops, and itching is common due to the reaction of the human body to the foreign protein in the louse's saliva. The continual itching, which is worse at night, can lead to secondary infections if the lice infestation is not treated.

Working out how to catch the lice without damaging them was the challenge. If a small animal has lice, it is possible to place it in a well-sealed plastic bag with its head free, and to pump chloroform into the bag. Once anaesthetised or dead, the lice fall off the animal and can be collected carefully from the inside of the bag. Yaco and Lucho discussed this method but realised the only way to do this would be using a bag specifically designed for a human body. Recognising that asking questions in town about how to acquire a body bag might create even more problems, they pondered on alternatives. Each louse would need to be placed in ethanol to preserve it, and then mounted on a microscope slide. Improperly prepared specimens are of no use to museums, and certainly would not earn any money, so they knew they needed to take the utmost care. So slowly and carefully, wearing headlamps to illuminate Pichi's infested pubes, they used a paintbrush dipped in ethanol to paint each louse. They needed to be very careful with the ethanol, as it can cause itching and inflammation on the skin, and also inhalation can affect the lungs and cause central nervous system damage. So Lucho painted abstemiously, and Yaco used tweezers gently to pull each louse free of its grasp on the hair. Given the size of the adult louse ranges from 1.25 to two millimetres, and that juveniles are much smaller, this was back-breaking work which took all night and part of the next day. The yield, however, was spectacular: ninety-two males, 140 females, and 337 juveniles. The mounting of these specimens onto slides took two more days, and then the specimens were packaged up and sent off to the Smithsonian. A fortnight later, a cheque arrived for just over $700, and Yaco was despatched to take it to Pichi.

But Pichi would not accept it. He knew his mother and siblings would be suspicious if he suddenly had money, and he was too ashamed to even want to think about ways of keeping it. He waved Yaco away and told him he could keep the money and do whatever he liked with it.

Yaco did not know what to do with the money either. He did not want to spend the proceeds of his brother's ill-fated affair on himself, and if he bought something for his own family, his wife would certainly want to know where he obtained that much money. In the end, he ordered a couch and two chairs with elaborate arms, something he knew his mother had always wanted in the family's small wooden house. Pichi happened to be home on the day the couch arrived by truck. His mother was absolutely thrilled, and told Pichi, 'You need to work hard like your brother. 'See how generous he is!'

The spirits in the trees

One of the animals that Peter was particularly interested in trapping was *Dromiciops australias*, recently renamed as *Dromiciops gliroides*. In Spanish, it is often called *monito del monte* or little monkey of the forest. So small they can fit into the palm of a human hand, these tiny nocturnal possums have the large soulful eyes common to possums everywhere. They also have long hairless prehensile tails which, like a monkey, they clearly use to good effect, as locals report seeing them in the winter and autumn, hanging from their tails outside their nests like ripe fruit in the sun.

Peter was keen to trap some of these opossums to examine their sperm, as sperm can sometimes tell a lot about the relationships between species. (For reasons beyond my comprehension, Australian possums are called possums and the South Americans call the same kinds of animals opossums). As a reproductive biologist, Peter had previously undertaken a lot of work on the sperm of Australian marsupials, and wanted to see whether the sperm structure of Australian possums was shared by a South American opossum.

Sperm develop in the male reproductive tract. They start their life as round cells in the testicles which divide and then develop into fully-formed sperm which are released into and move along a very long convoluted tube called the epididymis. It is during their passage through this long tube that the sperm develop their capacity to self-propel and thus to move to fertilise an egg. One of the advantages of using sperm to classify animals is that there is no need to sacrifice the animal to examine the sperm, as in many species of animals, sperm can be found in urine during mating season.

What is so fascinating about most American opossums is that the sperm join up to form precise head-to-head pairs in the epididymis. This complex rotation process to pair up with another sperm only happens in the very latter stages of their development in the epididymis. The pairs of sperm only separate after mating has taken place, and when they are very close to the egg. This phenomenon is thought to offer the sperm the best chance of reaching the egg and thus fertilising the female. In Australian possums, however, the sperm travel alone. Peter wanted to examine the sperm of the South American opossums to see if any of them also had sperm that travelled alone, as this would suggest a link to the Australian possums. Australia and South America were once all connected via the single land mass of Antarctica. In the same way that the *nothofagus beech* trees found in Tasmania and other Australian rainforests are descended from the *nothofagus* forests of Chile, a South American marsupial with the same sperm characteristics as Australian marsupials might also suggest a common ancestor.

To determine whether the sperm any of the South American opossums were identical to those of the Australian possums required examination of mature opossum sperm. Mature sperm are generally only found in animals during the breeding season. So the timing of a field trip to collect these animals was absolutely critical. And of course, fieldwork being conducted in one's own country can often suffer setbacks, as it can be hard to align all the factors necessary for a successful field trip. When the research is conducted overseas, in a different language, everything becomes even harder.

In 1983, Peter and his colleague and our close friend Dr Tom Grant had gone to Chile to attempt to trap *monitos* and the Chilean long-nosed shrew opossum, *rhyncholestes raphanurus*, from the Valdivian temperate rain forests of southern Chile. They were successful in trapping some males of both species in August and September, which they had guessed might be the breeding season. However, while there were signs of sperm development in these animals, no mature sperm had yet formed. Although that trip was not successful in answering the question about whether sperm of these South American opossums were paired or not, it had provided a lot of important information about the animals' habitat, trapping them and ways of working in the field, all of which were critical for the success of this subsequent trip.

From Peter and Tom's earlier visit, we knew that the *monitos* made distinctive nests in the forests, usually at least two metres from the ground, and that it was unlikely that they would venture into the traps set for them. So one technique of animal collection that they had trialled successfully was to go through the local inhabitants, among whom woodcutting was a common occupation. By distributing fliers with a photo of a *monito*, and above, the question, in Spanish, 'Have you seen this animal?' Peter and Tom had had some success in acquiring animals. Many woodcutters believe a *monito* to be a good spirit of the forest, which will bring wealth and good health to the captor. This myth has perhaps arisen because when a tree is felled, sometimes an apparently 'dead' monito falls to the ground. If a woodcutter runs to pick it up and warms it in his hands, it magically revives. Several locals told us they had found a *monito* [5] and taken it home, but because they believed it to be a spirit, they had offered it neither food nor water, and so the animal died. We had the opportunity to view animals in this state of inactivity or torpor, which enables them to survive under conditions of reduced food availability, as we eventually caught or acquired many animals, often from locals who had spread the word that we were looking for them.

Once the first local man brought in some animals, we set up a little cage for them and began making observations. The *monitos* weighed between twenty and thirty grams, and their tails were about ten centimetres long. When in torpor, the animals resemble a furry ball with the tail curled tightly around them. They are very cold to the touch, their eyes and ears are fast shut, and their ears are completely drooped. As they warm up and you attempt to free them from the confines of the ball shape, they unclench and clench their paws, and they open their mouth in a vague useless biting action while remaining motionless elsewhere. The tail persists in rolling back up, even if you unroll it. Watching these animals move in and out of torpor was fascinating. On the earlier trip, Tom Grant had taken measurements of the skin temperature of *monitos* as they went in and out of torpor, and written up the data for a chapter in a zoological book (Grant and Temple-Smith, 1987).

By the end of October, we had acquired eight females and nineteen males. Using very fine calipers, the length of each animal's head, tail, foot and ear was measured, and it was weighed in a sock using a handheld scale. For males, the scrotal width and depth were also measured. Distinctive colouring was recorded. Number 4, for example, was a female with a ginger patch below her ears, and a pouch ridge only, suggesting she had not had any pouch young. In contrast, Number 3 had a visible pouch area and large nipples, suggesting she had reproduced at least once before. To distinguish one *monito* from another, Peter gave each individual a specific identity mark by drawing lines on their tails with black marking pen. The pattern for each animal is recorded in the field notes. I was very relieved we ended up using this method, as I am reminded by my handwriting in the notes that an earlier attempt to label individuals by earmarking with a pattern of needlepoints failed, as the ears are so thin that the skin around the hole shrivelled up around it. I remember being glad this failed, as I felt it worried that these animals might suffer, even if only for a moment. Interestingly, Peter said he thought that there may well not be many nerves in that area of the ear, and if the animal's behaviour was anything to go by, they certainly did not react in any way to the needle. In any case, the hole in the ear of the test animal seemed to have grown over in a day or so.

Always a people-watcher, in the absence of any people to watch I focused on the animals. One of my self-appointed tasks was to make observations of their behaviour, which I found endlessly fascinating. For example, my notes from 22 October detailed one female's adjustment on being transferred from the tin in which she was delivered to us, to her new cage.

2.30 p.m. Very quick, active, furious. Bit Peter's finger with a head down action, steadying her grip with her two paws. A piece of apple was placed in the cage, she licked it first, then ate it by scraping her teeth over the top of it. Top of her mouth steady, lower jaw moves towards it. Ate for a while, then more exploration. Spent some time sitting on top of the sock – she likes surveying the world from there.

The *monitos* were generally quite active at night. Another note labelled 'Middle of night' was probably written on a night when I was unable to sleep from the cold. The note said,

rushes around at about 1000 km/hr. Around cage, up and down and round and round on the wire surface. Then went into torpor during the night, it was so cold.

In common with other marsupial possums, Peter expected that the *monitos* would like fruit and small insects. We fed them apples, bananas, boiled eggs (it was clear they liked the yolks) and crickets.

One of the locals had also brought in a long-nosed Chilean shrew opossum. It had been found under a log and was brought to us in an old tin can with holes punched in the lid. It was difficult to see the poor thing huddled in the can, and Peter was worried that he might be hungry and dehydrated so we quickly transferred the little animal into a holding cage.

In my pencilled handwriting in the field notes, I wrote that

as Peter attempted to place him in the cage head first, he splayed out his back feet to prevent this. So Peter put him into a sock and then put the sock into the cage. After a few seconds, the shrew opossum came out of the sock to explore the cage. He moved slowly, sniffing the air. Peter placed a dish with some wet gauze in it inside the cage, and the shrew opossum sat there for a very long time – almost 10 minutes- drinking the water. He left the dish for a few seconds only, and then mostly just sat in the dish and sniffed the air. Then he then drank again. Finally he deposited two faeces in the dish before withdrawing into the sock.

We placed a plate of worms in the cage for him. He didn't come out again until the light was off and the whole hut was completely dark. We could hear him exploring the cage and eating worms.

I recall how fascinating it was to watch the eating style of this animal, whom we named Max, on account of his fine whiskers. He used his front paws to hold the worm like humans hold a mug. Firstly, he would find the head end of the worm and bite it off, and then eat the worm bit by bit, using his back teeth for chomping, and the front teeth for drawing out the sinew of the worm. Chomp, chomp, chomp, then he would raise his head and have a good chew. If he dropped the worm for any reason, he always picked it up again at the end closest to where the head had been. When he got to the grubby intestines of the worm, he would wipe his nose and mouth after every bite to get rid of any crumbs of soil.

By the second day, placid Max was happy to take worms fed to him through the wire of the cage. You could poke a worm through and Max would grab it with both paws, chomp his way through, and then go and sit on top of his sock and survey his world. We were becoming quite attached to him. When we woke on a particularly cold morning two days after he was brought in, he was lying on his side, barely alive, and he died a short time later. Poor Max.

We were all so sad. We had no idea of what had caused Max's death. While we had no way of knowing how long he had been in that tin before he had been brought to us, he had seemed satisfied with his cage and was eating and drinking without any obvious signs of distress. It really highlighted our responsibility for the lives of any animals that ended up in our care, and for the first time I realised that in relation to this aspect of the field trip, it might not all be plain sailing. I felt sad again about Max years later when Peter told me that recent observational studies on the shrew opossum suggested that they need to eat a massive volume of worms and insects each day to survive, as their diet contains very little protein. I remember there were many uneaten worms in his cage when he died, but I now wonder if Max starved through lack of variation in his diet.

Within two hours, Max's reproductive tract had been dissected out. Peter could see he was a sexually mature male, with the paired sperm which is typical of South American opossums. Max did not die in vain; he provided all kinds of information which could help the survival of not only his own species, but also other marsupials. Even knowing this, I was still upset. After two days of close observation, I had become attached to Max. As with the female mouse that had died in the trap on our first night, it was another warning that I needed toughen up.

Visiting Lago Chapo

Travelling as the only female among a group of males offered many indignities in relation to privacy, or rather lack of it, for the four months we spent away from civilisation. When we were in the A-frame hut at Puyehue where there was a flushing toilet, I had no power to insist on a seat-down policy as was the case at home, and given that everyone slept in one big room, it was impossible to turn the light on for nocturnal visits. This led to a whole series of unfortunate incidents ranging from my sitting straight into the befouled toilet bowl to walking barefoot on someone else's floor splash. I began trying to hold on until daylight.

When we were outside laying traps in the wet forest, I resented the ease with which the men casually unzipped their fly anywhere they happened to be. I would take a wee in a panicked rush, remembering how my father-in-law after a picnic near a Tasmanian forest had once had a leech crawl up his wooden leg and attach itself to his penis. Making life more difficult for toilet activities, I often wore several layers of clothing carefully tucked in to my army disposal khaki pants to keep my bottom and thighs warm in the freezing temperatures. To avoid any potential leech situation, I looked for open clearings and sunny places, but as the weather became warmer in Chile, we soon found that open clearings were populated by hoards of horseflies (tabanids) which prefer to fly in sunlight. They are large and agile in flight, and the females bite animals, including humans, to obtain blood. Worse still, the bites really hurt and leave a large reaction which can be itchy for weeks. They were so bad that Peter and I would accompany each other to take a poo and one would swat the flies off the other's nether regions, tactfully averting the gaze, while the doing was being done.

So I was a little relieved when Lucho suggested that Checho take Peter and me to visit some woodcutters who lived at Lago Chapo, about four hours south of Puyehue, to see whether they had caught any *monitos* for us. I was very pleased to go on this little trip, as I just wanted a change from the routine, and perhaps the chance to interact with some women.

I knew the trip could offer real difficulties in communication. We would be relying only on our Spanish, which, while improving, was by no means fluent and not even always accurate. Checho spoke no English, and there were many times we misunderstood each other. He always persisted in coming at a topic from different angles if he was unsure if we had grasped his full meaning, an excellent strategy to ensure that we understood. He was also a wonderful guide and always pointed out things he knew would be of interest to us, such as different plants which were poisonous, or which were considered to have therapeutic properties. He told me that the Indians use bees to sting the hands of rheumatism sufferers. He said it works on the hands but nowhere else on the body. He also claimed that a cure for travel sickness was to place sticking plaster in the shape of a cross over the navel, to cover it completely. He had tested this out himself during a very bumpy helicopter ride he took when filming for the *National Geographic*, and he had remained perfectly fine! Curiously, Lucho, who had been somewhat sceptical about this cure, said that on one occasion he had put sticking plaster over his own navel in preparation to travel on a very winding and rough road. Subsequently, the trip was cancelled and he completely forgot to remove the plaster. He said for the next few days he felt very strange all day and it wasn't until he remembered he was wearing the plaster and removed it that he felt better. That story was most interesting to me as it confirmed my suspicions that Lucho sometimes slept in his clothes!

Given my constant state of cold, the thought of travelling in the *camionetta* for several hours with the heating on and the chance of my body thawing out, was very attractive. As it transpired, the drive to Lago

Chapo in the *camionetta* certainly warmed me up, but the constant driving rain also meant it was damp and muggy and airless, and by the time we arrived at a small clearing in the forest, I was feeling out-of-sorts.

The house appeared to be newly built. As we pulled up, various young men appeared and greeted Checho. They were obviously all good friends, if back slapping was any indication. At one point while items were being unpacked from the car, Checho rapidly explained that there was an outside latrine pit, but the family were uncomfortable with us using it, so when we needed to use the toilet we would need to go across the unmade gravel road to the forest and find a tree.

We were invited to *passen adelante*, go inside and sit down. The Indian family of nine, which included five sons and two daughters, lived in a wooden hut the size of a quarter of an average Australian suburban house. The hut was lined with newspaper and flattened cardboard boxes to prevent the wind whistling through the gaps, and it had an old wood stove, which kept the house quite warm. An enamel basin stood inside a sink with a draining board, but there was no running water. Chickens, cats and dogs wandered at random in and out of the house. I noticed that one cloth was used for both washing dishes and wiping everything. Despite that, food preparation was fastidiously clean. There was a single small hand mirror on a hook in the kitchen, with a single comb hanging beside a single towel. It became clear that these were communal items, as I observed several family members at different times using them.

Luciana looked about sixteen, and she had a happy and chubby baby, who was perhaps ten-months old. The baby was clearly adored by all, and was handed from one family member to another. Checho later told me when I asked who the father was that it was *él trauco*, a mythical man of the forest who frequently inseminated young women who lived in secluded communities. Lucho later mentioned that in some areas, *el trauco* was a convenient way of explaining births resulting from unplanned teenage pregnancies.

Once we were seated, Luciana put the baby in another room, and then returned to offer us maté, a beverage we soon came to love. Many Chilean rural homes constantly keep the kettle on the boil. Hot water is poured into a cup-sized dried gourd, which is sometimes decorated with silver. Tea is added to the cup, and the liquid is drunk through what can only be described as a very elaborate silver drinking straw, which has a perforated bulb at one end to prevent the tea leaves from entering the straw. The curious thing is not the container and straw, however, but the manner of drinking, as all those present take one sip, and pass the maté along to the next. It established the kind of camaraderie one feels, I imagine, when sharing communion wine in church, or a joint at a party. There was something very soothing about the maté ritual, once one had overcome the initial instant panic at the thought of germ-sharing with strangers.

Many years later during a work visit to Chile, I had the chance to reflect on other welcoming ways of Chilenos. Chilenos greet everyone with a kiss and hug, whether they be a prince or a pauper. In Australia, like the UK, a handshake is a common formal greeting in business. But there is something about a more intimate touch which encourages me to let down my guard.

As soon as we had started sharing the maté, Checho and everyone else but Luciana suddenly all disappeared outside. There were many long silences as we tried hard to communicate with her in Spanish, a language native to none of us. I was grateful to Peter for his presence and his persistence as the silences would been unbearably long if it had been just the two of us girls. She made bread from scratch and by the time she had fried it and put it on a plate in front of us with a cup of coffee, more than two hours had passed. Luciana's sister Adriana and their parents suddenly appeared, and they all stood and watched us eat while we were seated at the tiny table. It wasn't until later that I realised there were only three chairs. As it became pitch-black outside, a few candles were lit so we could see each other. Hours later, the remaining family members came in. We had no idea of what they had been doing, but I felt cross with Checho for leaving us for so many hours with no word of explanation. I expected that he was really just having a good catch-up with his friends, while Peter was waiting to ask the young men about their work and the animals they saw.

I felt so uncomfortable and cross that I went to bed in the back of the *camionetta* quite early. It was horrid. Within thirty minutes, a heavy downpour began which kept up all night. The windows had fogged up with my breath, and now rain was running in little rivulets down on the inside. It was steamy and stuffy and cold all at once, and I could hear all the others talking and laughing until the small hours. I was cold, and hungry, I felt homesick and lonely, and I wished Peter would come to bed. For the first time, I began to seriously doubt my wisdom in coming on the trip. I felt completely dependent on Peter whose Spanish was much better than mine. I was cross with him that he seemed to be having a fine time without me, and that he was probably now talking and drinking with Checho and the other men. Maybe they were even having more food! I wondered whether he saw me as a burden, even though I hadn't noticed him making allowances for or missing out on anything because of me.

I also thought of Luciana, and how she probably found the situation just as uncomfortable as me. Her future may have already been mapped out by her status as the young mother of a baby of unknown paternity living in a remote area. Keeping house for her family may have been her only option, and my observation was that that meant she was entirely at the beck and call of the men in the household.

It struck me that I was also at the beck and call of my husband, even though I had chosen to come on this field trip. My idealised – and, in retrospect, immature – view of marriage was that partners would always want to share adventures, and in reality I expected that those adventures would be likely to be initiated by Peter, who was far more adventurous than me. So despite my education and age, I still saw myself as dependent on him, and was largely content to follow his suggestions and requests. Maybe I had more in common with the young Indian woman than I thought. And what's more, despite all of the opportunities my life so far had offered, I must admit I felt a pinprick of envy seeing the unconditional love that shone from the baby's eyes when she gazed at her young mother.

The next morning was my birthday, and I woke up alone. Although I woke up damp and cold and stiff, I lay a while wondering what this birthday would be like. It would certainly be different from any other birthday I had ever had. I wondered where Peter was. Outside, there was no one to be seen. I was busting to go to the loo. I had to pull on my wet boots and stagger over the road to the forest to find a tree to hide behind. On my return to the car, Checho appeared and asked me if I wanted a wash, and I felt momentarily cheered by the thought of some warm water in a basin. But disappointingly he took me to the river, where I stood in the rain wondering what he expected me to do. I saw wet washing – several man-sized woollen socks and a threadbare cotton baby napkin lying in the drizzling rain on the green tussocky grass at the edge of the river, where the bank was slightly less steep. I remember being struck by several things. Imagine the discomfort of doing the washing on that slippery steep bank. How could it be done without losing balance and falling into the water? Was all the washing done in that icy fast-flowing water? How did their hands stand the cold? It certainly explained the reason that while the Indians always looked beautifully clean personally, their clothes were often filthy. I washed my hands and face, a somewhat awkward one-handed face splash while clinging onto the overhanging grass, and the water was so cold my hands and face remained red for ages afterwards. Checho leaned into the river and scooped up a large pot of water which he took inside for drinking and cooking. I remember wondering whether there were rules about exactly where the washing and water collection were done to prevent contamination, and resolved not to drink any water unless it had been thoroughly boiled!

I followed Checho inside the house. Adriana and Luciana were there with Peter, and they busily prepared what proved to be a very satisfying breakfast for us of scrambled eggs and diced ham, and a cup of milky coffee. We were then bundled into the *camionetta*. Peter said we were to visit the site where the brothers were felling trees. Adriana and two of her brothers also came with us, and sat, rather uncomfortably I am sure, in the tray boot. We drove thirty minutes through winding, unmade roads in relentless rain, until we reached the side of a lake.

It then became clear that to reach our destination we had to row a boat, in the rain, across a lake. I still had no clear idea of why we doing it. It was eerie; silent but for the splashing of the rain which fell through a swirling mist. It took thirty minutes to get to the other side. After clambering ashore, we climbed a hillside for about two kilometres to the wood-cutting area. The trail wound steeply up through boot-sucking mud. The constant rain made it incredibly slippery, and we were all saturated. Communication was made more difficult by the fact that these Indians spoke a particular dialect of Spanish which was almost impossible for Peter and me to understand. We were completely dependent therefore on Checho's ability to translate between our poor Spanish and this other dialect, as he spoke no English. We were able to make out that beneath the roots of an enormous felled tree the woodcutters had found two shrew opossums – one had run away, and the other had travelled many miles in a tin can to Puyehue. So this was where Max had been found! Now the day's long trip all made sense!

Peter took many photos of the site. The rich brown earth, still clinging to the massive tree roots, suggested great potential for future farming in the area, but we both felt sobered by the wide destruction of the massive trees before us. The drizzle continued relentlessly, and after an hour or so, everyone became cold. We slid precariously back down the mountainside through the giant obstacle course created by the enormous felled trees in various stages of being cut by handsaws, and rowed back across the lake in the drizzle.

On the way back to our hosts' house, we stopped at what looked like an Indian house, but turned out to be the equivalent of the local store, with just a few items on shelves for sale. We bought a frozen chicken and a bag of flour. On our arrival back at the house, once again Peter and I were ushered inside to sit on the chairs, while the cooking was done. Adriana and Luciana prepared *sopaipillas,* a kind of delicious fried bread. They boiled the chicken and served it first as a soup, then pieces of chicken were served with rice and potatoes as main course. I was acutely aware that the single chicken was shared amongst twelve.

After dinner, there was the sound of someone clapping outside. This is apparently the standard alternative to a doorbell in rural Chile, and possibly other parts of the world. A local man entered, followed by several more. They came to watch the tiny battery-powered TV, which was screening a football game between Chile and Argentina. Once the match was over, we drove one of the sons of the house into Puerto Mont. We then had a further three hours to drive home. Checho drove, and Peter dozed, and I wondered what all my family would be doing and whether they were missing me on my birthday. Although I had not expected any greetings or gifts, it was probably the first time in my life that my birthday had gone by almost completely unacknowledged, although Peter had wished me happy birthday as we ate breakfast. We eventually arrived at Puyehue at eleven thirty p.m., in pouring rain.

To my surprise, the A-frame hut was in darkness. As I opened the door, though, I could see a single candle alight on the kitchen table. Beside it was a birthday cake! It was topped with a little homemade wax kangaroo candle, holding a tiny card in an envelope. When extracted, the card said '*Feliz Cumpleanos,* happy birthday'. The icing was decorated with puffed wheat. I was very touched that Lucho and Pedro had gone to this trouble for me, and we all enjoyed a slice of cake before getting into bed.

Next morning, we had birthday cake for breakfast, other food being in short supply. And much as I appreciated their efforts with the cake, I ungratefully and grumpily wished they had made less effort with the cake and had instead gone to secure some real food for breakfast. This was probably the morning that Pedro and Checho decided to call me *Meni meni,* which they said means 'good morning' in Araucani, their native language, apparently because they had observed that morning was not my best time of day.

To Argentina with contraband

In addition to searching for *monitos* in Chile, Peter had another quest. He was interested in the Patagonian opossum, a small carnivorous marsupial called *Lestodelphys halli*, of which very little evidence had ever been found at that time and no live specimens had been caught for over fifty years. Thirty years later, in 2015, the *Handbook of the Mammals of the World* lists this species as having 'a wide distribution, presumably a large population, and occurs in several protected areas. There are no major conservation threats to the Patagonian opossum, although some populations are threatened by habitat modifications by humans'. But in 1985, that was not known, so Peter was keen to see if he could find a living specimen. We only had limited time available as he was due to start work in London in January, so there was some indecision about how long we should stay in Chile in the hopes of the monitos becoming reproductively mature, and when we should head to Argentina.

In late October, when it became clear from the *monitos'* behaviour – or, more explicitly, lack of behaviour – that it was not yet their breeding season, we were faced with the prospect of waiting for an unknown period of time. Peter did not want to operate on an animal to extract the sperm he needed unless it was evident from its behaviour towards females that it was capable of mating. So he decided to wait, and use the intervening time to search for the Patagonian opossum. There was only one problem. We needed to continue to observe the behaviour of the *monitos*, and also check their urine regularly for sperm. Known as spermatorrhoea, sperm in urine is a natural phenomenon in male marsupials in breeding condition, and it could help to indicate the peak of male fertility. So there was nothing else we could do but to take the *monitos* with us and monitor their progress. Clearly, taking all of the animals which we now had in our colony would be very difficult, so we released all but five before we travelled to Argentine Patagonia at the start of November. We would then be able to release the five at their site of capture when we returned to Chile in late December, by which stage surely the breeding season would have been reached!

We were uncertain whether the soldiers who guarded the border between Chile and Argentina would have any instructions on animals being carried between the two countries. The decision was made by Lucho and Peter that we should not declare them given that we intended to take the animals straight back into Chile at the end of our Argentinian stay. Lucho said that if the soldiers took them, they would most likely kill them or release them, which would also mean death in an unfamiliar environment. So the travelling *monitos* were hidden in a pair of thick Explorer brand socks as we passed over the border into Argentina, and also again on the return to Chile.

Of course, the *monitos* felt like part of the family and I had given them all names – Gabriela, Caballero, Mauricio, Carlito and Carolina. The travelling *monitos* were subsequently weighed and measured every week or so, and their individual bodyweights were plotted on a graph so we could be sure they remained healthy. Using a travelling microscope, the urine of the males was checked regularly for sperm.

The day we left Puyehue National Park was sunny, only the second clear day after more than two weeks. As we drove higher and higher up steep roads and around and over hills which in parts were completely nude of vegetation, we caught glimpses of the volcano known as Volcan Osorno. Driving even higher through Antillanca, we began to pass through swirling mists through which there were glimpses of blue sky. We had no trouble crossing the border at Los Pajaritos, despite Lucho's anxiety that our array of chemicals and glassware might look like terrorist equipment. The soldiers barely even looked at the vehicles or the equipment or even Peter, who had the socks with five sleeping *monitos* deep in the pocket of his trousers. Despite our careless bantering about the 'smuggling' of these animals both from and back into Chile, I had been anxious about this border crossing, so it was a relief to be through.

I had also been dry-mouthed and sweaty-palmed at the thought of crossing the Andes, which I imagined might involve roads barely clinging to steep cliffs above plunging precipices, so I was very relieved when the road turned out to be a gentle climb over a wide pass. As we got closer to the snowy volcano caps, the trees became sparser, and once over the pass, the scenery was breathtaking. Huge silent, still lakes reflected the snowy mountain range, and in the foreground were bright orange and yellow flowering bushes. The forest trees were still enormous, but the undergrowth was less dense, and in some places grass alone formed the understorey, giving the appearance of a large well-tended parkland.

We camped one night on the beach of a lake, Lago Villarino, surrounded by mountains. The water was so clear you could see five metres or more to the bottom of the lake. We built an enormous fire and roasted potatoes under a sky so starry it seemed ablaze with light. Next morning, there was swirling mist as far as the eye could see, and washing in the icy lake was sheer torture.

As we climbed higher in the mountains, around every bend in the road was a blue, glassy lake, reflecting a series of perfect snowy peaks. Eventually, we stopped gasping and commenting on the views, as it seemed trite. At the pretty little town of San Martin de los Andes, we met up with the director of the Instituto Patagonia de Sciencias Naturales, Mario Gentili. He kindly offered us the use of a Swiss-style cottage for the night, and I was in heaven, as there were sheets on the bed! He also invited us to see his museum, which included an interesting insect collection.

Subsequently, he gave hundreds of specimens of beetles to Lucho to take away to identify, as Lucho was reknowned as a world-leading coleopterist, or beetle specialist. Lucho had literally discovered hundreds of new species of beetles in his career, and often, after examining the insects collected during the day, he would select out some of them and announce, with endearing enthusiasm, 'Each one new, new!'

Mario gave us our first experience of a home-made Argentinian-style *asado* (barbecue) which took place in the Andes, at the edge of a beech forest. We ate salami, chorizo, cheese and bread while we waited for the (other) enormous piece of meat to cook. It was apparently the flap of meat from between the ribs. Heavily salted, it was both absolutely delicious and impenetrably tough, which may explain why it needed to be eaten gaucho-style. This involved impaling one end of a strip of meat on a stick. With the other end of the strip of meat between the teeth, a knife was used to hack through the meat.

Luckily, my father could not see my efforts. He had a terror of me mishandling knives which lasted until his death at eighty-eight. He believed I was not to be trusted, and he must have somehow communicated halfway across the world to our host, who, when he saw my feeble efforts, offered to use his knife to cut my strip of meat while it was between my teeth. I felt a bit like an audience member hauled onstage to be the target for a knife-throwing act. It was one of those many moments on the trip when I rapidly considered the ramifications of offending my host. Given that he had offered to let us use the Instituto's accommodation, which had a bathroom with hot water, I literally gritted my teeth and allowed him a single knife swipe. Fortunately, the morsel of meat was so chewy that when he offered to do it again I was able to say I was still busy eating, and when he wasn't looking I slipped my remaining meat into the coals of the fire. As there never seemed to be any salad or vegetables at an *asado,* there was no need for plates. Dessert was a slice of cheese topped with *dulce de papas,* a firm jelly made of sweet potatoes, rather cloyingly sweet. As we went to our accommodation, I was craving lettuce and celery and cucumber and tomatoes, but when I climbed into clean sheets I was so grateful to our host for that luxury that I would have gladly eaten nothing but *asado* every day for a week!

I had never expected to find both chocolate box views *and* chocolate in South America, so the famous dark chocolate with almonds (*chocolate con almendras*) was our companion over the next couple of days and as we drove onto Bariloche. There, a well-known near-retired American zoologist, Oliver Pearson, from the University of California at Berkeley, was staying with his wife, as they did every year. We had dinner with them, which was so nice for me. Anita was the first woman with whom I had conversed in English for many weeks. When I confessed that Peter's snoring was keeping me awake wherever we slept, she suggested that I try to turn it into a positive emotion, and instead of being cross I should feel grateful that I had this wonderful man next to me. I tried the strategy when we returned to our campsite at Lago Nahuel Haupi. It didn't work. Then or ever.

The next morning, Lucho, Checho and Pedro were busy setting up insect traps, and Peter and I drove the *camionetta* alone into town. We sat in a café and had a toasted sandwich and coffee, while writing letters home. What a treat to be a normal tourist for a day! That's when I felt grateful for the wonderful man beside me...

Patagonia

Finally, after descending the mountains and leaving the beautiful Bariloche, we glimpsed the real Patagonia – miles and miles of dry gullies and huge straggly mountains, where squat flowering shrubs and scrubby bushes characterised by a myriad of spines were constantly blown about. This provided a shifting colour contrast against a vista of ochre, grey and dusky green. The wind – strong, relentless, and stinging with grit – provided a challenge for almost everything. Any activity undertaken outside became potentially treacherous as there was no way to predict when the gusts would start or cease.

After the first day, everyone was complaining of headaches and neck-aches from walking with jaws clenched and shoulders hunched. The winds were so forceful that one could actually 'sit' in the wind by leaning back and allowing the wind to take your body weight. This was exhilarating for the first few hours while we were being buffeted as we admired the view. Stretching in every direction were miles of low open grasslands severed only by glacier-fed crystal clear rivers, framed against distant mountains. The first man in the group who tried to take a wee in this glorious scene reported problematic splashback following poor judgement of wind direction. When I tried to follow suit, not only was I aware that there were no trees or shrubs over eighteen inches to hide behind, but I absolutely could not hold myself steady in a squat. Even with Peter bracing me, it was still difficult, as he was buffeted around too. Eventually he had to brace himself against the *camionetta* or campervan to support me while I took a wee, desperately trying to stem the flow when gusts of wind swirled under or around the vehicle.

On one occasion, we drove past what were clearly some new gates being erected at the entry to an estancia. These properties are so large that the farmhouse might be twenty kilometres from the gate. At the entrance to the property, in preparation for the gateposts some large holes had been dug, about three feet deep and three feet in diameter. This was a perfect crouching spot for me to use, and everyone was amused by my head only showing above ground height. It was such a relief to be able to squat without being blown over.

There are many police checkpoints throughout Argentina, and some feel as if they are in the middle of nowhere. At the El Balson checkpoint, a single boom gate crossed the road, manned by a single silent guard. I was impressed by his green uniform with red accents, and I asked if I could take his photo. Even though there was no one else for miles around to view his commitment or otherwise to his duty, he looked at me unblinkingly and moved his head sharply a fraction, indicating that I could not.

Many kilometres past the checkpoint, and towards the end of the day, the sky darkened, suddenly announcing the arrival of what proved to be an enormous storm. We camped by the river in the pouring rain, the first poor weather we had experienced since leaving Chile almost a month before. In the morning when we awoke, there was a horse, a man, a woman and several small children huddled around a fire near the vehicles. It seemed they had been making their way in the dark through the storm when they saw our campsite, and decided to seek shelter there.

In such a landscape where large herds of cattle graze in the huge unfenced estancias, or farms, one rarely saw another person. While at times we came across spectacular birds such as rheas, flamingos and lapwings, it was rare and difficult to spot any other animals, such as the huge hare-like rodent called a mara, amongst the low scrub. One blissfully windless day, we saw a distant puff of smoke and spent a great deal of time speculating on the cause. We realised that the puff seemed to be getting bigger, until eventually we could concentrate on nothing else other than the puff of grey smoke growing larger in the cloudless blue sky. It was sunny, cold and completely still. Suddenly, we heard two short sharp high-pitched noises echoing in the valley, and we realised that underneath the smoke must be the Old Patagonian Express train (La Trochita). It runs weekly on a narrow gauge rail for four hundred kilometres through the foothills of the Andes between the provinces of Chubut and Rio Negro. We had simply not been able to see the railway line in the scrub. The railway has been operational since 1935 and comprised an old-fashioned steam engine drawing two equally old-fashioned-looking carriages. There was no one on board apart from the train driver, who was clearly excited to see us. He waved a red flag and tooted his whistle as he passed by.

Later that same day, I walked far away from the campsite, relieved that the absence of wind meant I could relieve myself alone. I was on a slight rise, so I had a good view of the distant campsite and could see if anyone was headed my way. I was enjoying the sun on my bare bottom when I heard the whinny of a horse and looked to my right to see a lone rider staring at me. He was dressed as a typical gaucho – fancy saddle and spurs, wide-legged pants and red scarf around his neck, and a hat. I froze. We made eye contact. I didn't know what to do. I didn't want to stand up in case he hadn't noticed my pants were around my ankles, although in retrospect that seems highly unlikely since he was up high on a horse! For the longest time, he just stared without any change of expression. Eventually, he flicked the reins and he and the horse slowly ambled away from me and were swallowed by the pampas.

Later that day, we drove past some spectacular lakes alive with a seething mass of pink flamingos. As the road continued down the valley, we also passed large salt pans. I had the chance to study them, as every kilometre or two, Peter and Lucho, who were travelling in the *camionetta* in front of the camper, would stop to examine the insects that had been killed by hitting the windscreen of the cars. If they might be a new species, Lucho would want to save them carefully, noting down the place where they died, the weather conditions, the date and the name of the species if he knew it. While I enjoyed looking at the scenery, by the end of each day I felt exhausted by our incredibly slow progress and, once outside the vehicle, battling the ceaseless wind. On family holidays in the years to come, I would be reminded of Patagonia every time Peter pulled over the car to examine some native roadkill. At least in Australia, we were spared the wind.

In addition to the hazards posed by the wind and the trapping on the trip, scrabbling through the bush often resulted in injury. On two separate occasions in Chile, Peter accidentally was speared in the eye by a sliver of bamboo, and on both occasions the cut got infected. He was not an easy patient and would not stop work to rest. Eventually, I convinced him to wear an eyepatch to prevent other bits of dust and dirt flying into it. We all had insect bites or scratches that became infected but in general we managed pretty well given the rough circumstances of many of our activities.

Far more potentially serious was a point in the trip when we were as far away from medical help as we could possibly be, and Lucho suddenly complained of acute pain in his side. He was reasonably sure it was a kidney stone, as he had apparently had them before. Peter recalled on an earlier trip with Tom that Lucho had had a similar attack that lasted for several days and Peter eventually had to inject him with morphine to reduce the pain. It was truly dreadful to watch someone else's suffering at such close quarters, and gave me an inkling of how men must feel watching their partner in labour. Indeed, after labouring for many hours, Lucho's grey and sweaty face finally regained some colour as he announced the emergency was over, and that he had passed the stone. He slept through a day and night afterwards, and then was up and about again as if nothing had happened. But it was a reminder to me of just how vulnerable we were. While Lucho had an emergency kit, it was little better than what I carried in my handbag (or used to carry in my handbag, as I was no longer using one). What would happen if someone had a serious injury? It was too scary to contemplate.

My ability to imagine both the best and worst possible outcome to any event has been a pattern in my life. Over time, I have learnt to manage the associated low-grade anxiety by thinking through how I might manage any negative outcomes. Peter, who was once described by a friend as 'so laid-back, he's almost horizontal' often contributed to this anxiety through his ability to ignore potential hazards.

For example, many years ago on the last day of a holiday in Fiji, he went scuba diving. A few hours later, as the homeward flight took off, he mentioned to me the dangers of diving and flying on the same day, so I would know what to do in case he lost consciousness. (I had no idea what to do.) Quite recently, he called me from the Matterhorn. He was walking up high, alone, the weather was closing in, it was nearly dark, and he had three hours of walking to reach other people. He'd just thought he'd let me know. (Thanks.)

Over the years, he has white-water rafted, climbed scary mountains, swum with whales, been lowered in a cage to film white pointer sharks. He also likes driving interstate and sleeping by the road, riding his bike long distances and generally pushing himself physically. As I have got older, I realise that the only reason there are some people who can do these exciting things is because there are other people, like me, who not only provide the audience, but can be relied upon to pick up the pieces when required.

Looking for the Patagonian opossum

The Patagonian opossum is a carnivorous marsupial about the size of a small rat but with a heavy lower jaw and a fine set of teeth. A Mr T.H. Hall collected the first known specimen of *Lestodelphys halli*, although at that time, being the first specimen ever collected, it was unnamed. Such a specimen is known as a holotype, as it is the example upon which a new species is described. Mr Hall had captured the animal by accident in early July 'about 1920'. He had hung rhea meat above two feet from the ground to trap a fox, and he observed a small animal eating the meat. When it finished, it jumped down, unfortunately straight onto the fox trap. This event was recorded as having occurred at 'Estancia Madujada, not far from Puerto Deseado' (Thomas, 1929: 45). The specimen, strangely enough, was one of a collection sent to Perth Museum in Australia, and from there was traded to the British Museum.

Before the mid-1980s, very few samples of the Patagonian opossum had ever been collected. Peter had taken photos and descriptions of the skins and bones stored in the British Museum to assist us to correctly identify the animal if we happened to catch one. But before we headed down to the last known area of the Patagonian opossum habitat, Peter was keen to explore other parts of Argentina, to see whether he could add information to the known distribution of this animal. Oliver Pearson, with whom we had dinner in Bariloche, had advised Peter that some bones of the Patagonian opossum had been found many decades ago on an estancia called Los Manantiales, near Languineo. As it was between Bariloche and Puerto Deseado, it seemed sensible to stop to look for the Patagonian opossum on the way.

We had the map coordinates of Los Manantiales, so we headed in that direction, but were unable to find a road to Languineo. Later, we learned that it was a department area of the Chubut province, so there was not an actual town of that name. Once in the general region, on the very rare occasions we encountered a living person, who mostly seemed to be lone gauchos or elderly men with a dog, we asked if they had heard of an estancia called Los Manantiales. No one had. When we were about to give up hope, we came across a petrol station and went in there to ask. Also inside was a moustachioed man who appeared to be in his fifties, wearing a fine wool V-necked jumper, open-necked shirt with a cravat and a beret. As luck would have it, he turned out to be the nephew of the duenna, the lady owner of Los Manantiales. He invited us to his home. He clearly lived alone and was very keen for company. He invited us to sit in an impeccably clean and large kitchen with a wood-burning stove. He had no electricity, only paraffin lamps, so there was no fridge, only an old-fashioned meat safe. Over maté and dry biscuits, he told us a little about his family history, and then explained exactly how to find Estancia Los Manantiales.

We would never have found it without his help. Tucked away, miles from anywhere, the only sign was a cluster of trees just visible from the road. The lengthy avenue of poplars and willows suggested an estancia of some wealth, at least in the past if not present. The driveway ran alongside a gully with a fast-flowing creek. Eventually, we came to a row of adobe Indian huts, with some elderly Indians sitting on the porch by the light of paraffin lamps. And then a little further along was the estancia itself, built of brick with a flat roof. I remember being struck by the height of the windows. They started at my waist height and finished at my shoulder height. I wondered if it meant the occupants were tiny people, or had they once been at eye height and the ground around had sunk?

In the manner of country folk across the world, the duenna, Elfrida, welcomed us. Of German and Spanish origin, she had been managing the estancia alone since her husband died. Now in her seventies, she relied heavily on two Chilean Indian women who appeared to be in their sixties and an Indian teenager, who, judging by their deferential manner to her, were her employees. And they were all very short people, so quite possibly the window height had been made to order!

The estancia kitchen reminded me of an Australian kitchen from the 1930s. An iron wood-burning stove was constantly being fed with small logs. A plastic table cloth and plastic curtains suggested that attention was given to cleanliness, and indeed the floor was so clean you could have eaten off it. The kitchen dresser was painted green, and had old-fashioned push-in knobs to open the door and drawers. China dog ornaments reminded me of a pair my sister and I had been given as children by neighbour, of a white China poodle dressed as a bride (mine), and pink China poodle dressed as a groom (my sister's). I still have mine, although the painted details on the bridal train are fading.

While we were occupied with maté drinking, our attention was drawn to the framed set of Indian spearheads on the wall, which apparently had been found around the estancia. Elfrida's family had been there for generations, and she was proud to show us her museum – two rooms stuffed full of family memorabilia. Much of it, I judged to be worthy of a real museum. There were many Indian stone implements such as flechas or arrowheads, tanned capybara skins, coins, bones and fossils. There were also interesting personal items such as her grandfather's first pair of baby boots, his first riding whip, and many children's toys which had accompanied the family on their emigration from Europe two hundred years before. Elfrida's grandfather had found a fossil of a glyptodont on the estancia – a giant armadillo about eight feet long and five feet high.

In 1957, another brother had found the skull of the Patagonian opossum, which he had sent to the Buenos Aires Museum, and which subsequently made its way to the British Museum. Whether the animal had actually been living on the estancia or whether the skull had come from another place, though, she did not know. As we were looking at these items, dusk fell and I wondered why she didn't turn on the light to allow us to see better. It wasn't until I asked to use the bathroom that

I realised there was no electricity, as she gave me a lamp to light my way.

We had a delicious if unusual dinner with Elfrida that night. A chicken stew with onion and tomatoes on rice was served alongside home-made gnocchi with a beef sauce. After that, an *asado* of tough but tasty grilled meat was served with roast potatoes. The unusual combination had me worrying that the arrival of five strangers plus her nephew might have used up all her food supplies. For dessert, we had Chilean peaches, which I found to be far superior to the Australian ones, although perhaps that was because up until then there had been a fruit drought in our diet for a period of weeks. She kindly offered Peter and me a bed inside for the night, but we politely declined. She was happy for us to park the campervan and *camionetta* in her yard overnight, although I found it difficult to find somewhere to go to the toilet once we had all retired. Every time I set a foot outside the campervan, the dogs started a wild barking which echoed through the valley.

Elfrida gave us permission to camp on her property, so the next day we drove a further thirty kilometres or so on from the homestead and set up camp in a dry gully with only a trickle of water flowing through. Battling with the massive gusty winds and spiny vegetation, we laid traps and checked them two to three times per day, re-baiting if necessary. We all became severely windburnt, and everything we ate was gritty and tasted of sand. As soon as the sun rose, the wind rose, and yet the nights were incredibly peaceful and starry. Unfortunately, the nights were also bitterly cold, so while it would have been pleasant to lie on the ground to stargaze, it was far too uncomfortable to do so.

All along the valley, we searched high in the cliffs for signs of owls, clearly evident by white streaks of excrement on the rockface. Owls are likely to eat an animal the size of the Patagonian opossum. They are unable to digest the fur and bone of their prey, which they usually swallow whole, so the undigested parts are coughed up several hours after feeding in what is known as an owl pellet. After each night's hunting, an owl generally regurgitates one or two pellets. Evidence of owl occupation of caves high in rocky outcrops was both in the white markings made by their excrement, and in the nearby piles of pellets, which looked to me like dried faeces of a bigger animal. As we walked about, laying traps, any time we saw owl pellets, we collected them in plastic bags and labelled the bag with the location. At night, we spent hours dissecting the pellets to extract the bones from the fur. The bones were always completely devoid of any vestige of flesh, testimony to the efficient functional properties of the owl's digestion. It was like a mini archeological dig, with every pellet unveiling its secret as it was carefully dissected. I enjoyed it, although the dried fur sometimes made me sneeze, and I secretly worked hard in the hopes that I would be the one to discover some sign of the Patagonian opossum in 'my' pellets. I achieved a small success, as recorded in Peter's field notes:

> 7.11.85 Using Pearson's suggestions re white markings along cliff face – heavy grazing by sheep and horses into cliffs – also evidence of hares – dead sheep – evidence of mountain vizcachas (small rodents which look like chinchillas) – collected large quantities of owl pellets from two main sites in the cliffs about ½ km apart. High winds, exposed site but deposit zone in a deep crack in the cliff face. Large numbers of owl pellets collected, more from the first site with Checho, MT-S and PT-S. Also in first site and to a lesser extent in the second, were large numbers of bones from degraded owl pellets. MT-S found a pellet with part of a maxilla (upper jawbone) of a small carnivore…? Patagonian opossum (pellet subsequently dissected and bones saved). PT-S found a mandible (lower jawbone) with all the features of a Patagonian opossum. Pellets all to be dissected, matched with trapped specimens.

In addition to looking for the owl pellets, we also set traps in the hopes of catching a live Patagonian opossum. Again, from the field notes on 7.11.85:

> Line of cage traps up the hillside baited with meat, and two lines of Elliots baited with either meat or Quaker (oats). Meat has its problem as bait – dried quickly, hardened, lost odour and attracted ants, but we should persist since Budin's Patagonian opossums were

taken with rhea meat baited traps. One line of Elliots going up to beneath the cliff had fifty-three traps, the second line covering the lower portion of the hill had thirty Elliots, also eleven Elliots near the river on the flat.

The entry for the following day noted that those traps had yielded twelve captures, all rodents, of four different species. All animals were weighed, measured and photographed. The second nail on the left foot was also cut, so that any recaptures on subsequent nights could be identified. All animals were then released. At seven p.m., the traps were all checked, rebaited and reset, and then it was back to the camp to work on dissecting the pellets. We were always busy.

Peter, Checho and I were driving in the *camionetta* one day when I noticed something run across the track in front of us, which disappeared into the scrub as we drove by. When I pointed it out to Checho, he braked sharply, yelled at Peter to grab the steering wheel and, with the *camionetta* still moving, he jumped out and dived into the scrub. Moments later, he emerged with a squirming armadillo which he thrust into my hands. He shouted that they always travelled in pairs, and that we should follow him in the car, and he ran off to see if he could find another one. It was a real struggle to hold the armadillo – I had no idea they would be so strong. The thin bony plates across the armadillo's back, head and tail meant I had to grasp the unprotected body beneath the shell, while avoiding the strong digging claws. I soon became exhausted struggling to hold the armadillo and so Peter stopped the *camionetta* and took over, and not long after, Checho returned with another. He put them in the back of the *camionetta*, so we could take photos and show them to the others.

Although books say that armadillos are generally solitary creatures that spend sixteen hours a day sleeping and only interact to mate, these two seemed to be the best of friends. Their highly developed sense of smell and long sticky tongues enabled them to catch insects hidden in foliage or under logs, and because they have poor eyesight, they didn't seem to notice me watching them. Over the next day, I really enjoyed their company in between catching insects for the travelling *monitos*, laying and checking traps, and dissecting owl pellets.

One afternoon, I returned to the campsite after having done some washing a kilometre away next to a cattle trough. It was hard work, requiring a bucket and a basin and a very low threshold for cleanliness, given the level of grit in the wind and the likely level of cattle saliva in the trough, which I braced myself to ignore. I washed our socks and underwear in the bucket of water with a little detergent, and emptied it into the sand, aghast at the absolute filth which emerged. I did another soapy wash before rinsing the items twice in the dusty cattle trough water and struggling back against the wind. It was only later when I got back to the campsite that Peter told me the socks I washed included the befouled travelling *monito* sock! So in addition to grit and cattle spit, my underwear was also coated in microscopic *monito* poo. I tried to repress my feeling of disgust, but that was the point where I gave up on trying to maintain some standard, and became, figuratively speaking, one of the boys.

But there was worse to come. When we sat down to dinner that night, it was a stew made from sinewy meat which tasted a bit like wild duck. I chewed a bit of the leg but mostly ate just the gravy. When I looked over at Peter's plate, I realised with horror that he was eating the cooked head of an armadillo, with eyeballs intact! It was hard not to burst into tears. While I had been away from the camp, washing, Checho had seized the chance to provide us with meat and to provide himself with two armadillo shells which he said he could sell to a music shop, where they would be made into the small guitars called charangos.

Unreasonably, I blamed myself for the deaths of the animals, firstly by initially spotting one and then by being absent when their fate was sealed. I was so upset that I was not even sympathetic when Peter, who had asked Checho for the testes of the male so he could dissect them, found the cooked testes served up alongside the head for his dinner. The others watched him expectantly all through dinner, to see if he had the cojones (Spanish for 'balls') to eat them. He did.

I went to bed sad, tired of the men and their machismo, and missing the company of my family and friends, who I felt sure would understand my feelings.

After several days of unsuccessful trapping, we left Los Manantiales and began the very spectacular drive along the Chubut River Valley to the coast of Patagonia. The Chubut River was wide and fast-flowing and offered lots of opportunity for freezing cold washes. The strata in the distant rock faces were so clear they almost appeared to have been painted, and the wind had eroded the cliffs into fascinating shapes. We often stopped to climb up to the top of cliffs to collect owl pellets which were both inside and outside the caves. In some places, piles of disintegrated pellets signalled that an owl had moved elsewhere, perhaps because of another predator entering the area. I always did my collecting quite warily in such places. We were standing on such steep slopes, and although I had no idea of what predator I expected might emerge from the cave, I could imagine myself hurtling down the hillside being chased by something with teeth. I expect it was just the vast emptiness that felt unfamiliar. We drove miles and miles through such endless pampas bounded only by the high cliffs which marked the path of the prehistoric river.

The downside to travelling through this spectacular scenery was the difficulty we had in sourcing food for the travelling *monitos*. The combination of high winds and sparse low scrub meant insects remained absent or well-hidden. Sunsets were spectacular, but the moment the magnificent colours in the sky paled, dusk fell and the wind died. Lucho would set up his insect-attracting lights and we would take turns to stand guard with the butterfly nets to try to capture moths. Moths do not have a lot of substance in terms of protein, so to keep the *monitos* well-fed meant a lot of moth catching. It was tiring work.

However, the low point of the trip food-wise for the humans came in Argentina several days after Lucho reluctantly left his insect collecting at my request to scout for villages or farms from which to procure fresh food. We were all feeling constantly tired from a diet which lacked any variation and was virtually exclusively carbohydrate. Curiously, I had noticed the effects of this poor nourishment firstly on the two Indian men, who became irritable and grumpy and excessively tired. Peter could also perceive the change when I pointed it out. Lucho soon followed suit, and I realised that it was likely one of those times when a lifetime of excellent nutrition holds you in good stead. When Lucho's food-foraging trip produced only two onions and a very limp carrot, he realised that food might need to become a priority. He said he would prepare dinner that night and I, at least, was looking forward to a one-fifth share of a carrot and two onions.

We sat down, unusually, to the campervan table set with cutlery and wine glasses and a paper towel serviette. My spirits rose as I realised that he had a surprise up his sleeve – I imagined that perhaps he had secretly managed to buy some meat and broccoli or tomatoes. When we were all seated, and with great gusto, Lucho served each of us an entire dinner-plate-sized mound of Deb instant mashed potato, with a garnish of sweet chilli sauce. He poured a pink opaque liquid into our wine glasses. It was a special South American cocktail, he said. It was red wine, mixed with powdered milk, and it was truly revolting. When we came to the realisation that, apart from oatmeal, this really *was* all the food we had left, I felt quite angry, and then almost tearful. After all, this was the reason we had paid someone with regional knowledge, so we didn't get into such a situation! Lucho continued to make light of it and suggested we try to hunt for meat the next day, but I knew what he was really saying was 'Don't hold your breath in the hope that the situation will change soon.'

Over the next couple of days, we were hungry and I remained angry. I avoided Lucho. I must have looked particularly grim. Checho took me aside and told me I shouldn't worry, that he had a special gift for me, one that would keep me safe. It was the foot of the male armadillo, which he had dried and attached to a string. He insisted I wear it as an amulet around my neck. I still have that foot in my jewellery box. I must remember to tell my children what it is, as I'm sure they will have no idea if they find it after I am gone.

I have no recollection of when and how we finally obtained food, but I knew that Lucho would never dare to let supplies get so low again. That was the first time on the trip I felt I had gained some respect from Lucho. Perhaps it was the first time I had allowed myself to react like a woman, instead of trying to be one of the men.

Towards the sea

Our next destination was, surprisingly, one I chose. When I was at boarding school in Year 9, I wasn't doing so well at maths. I had moved school pretty much every two years, as my dad was transferred around Australia. All the moving meant I got used to being the new kid at school. All the states of Australia then had different curricula for school students, so while it seemed I learnt at every new school about Captain Cook 'discovering' an already populated continent, there were some things I missed out on everywhere.

When my maths teacher, Miss Mac, discovered I was in Year 9 and could not multiply and divide fractions, she was horrified. My parents were duly contacted and after she had gained their permission, she told me she was going to tutor me for one hour each week until I caught up with the rest of the class. She worked me hard. Fortunately, she recognised that I was not someone who performed well under pressure, and the week before the maths exam she told me to take the week off study and not worry. I must have had a pained expression on my face, as she went on to suggest that I get hold of a great book, and allow myself to get absorbed in it so I didn't fret about the exam. She asked if I had a such a book, and I must have said I didn't, for the next day after class she pulled me aside and handed me a little bundle of books which she thought might do the trick. She said if I got through them before the exam, she could bring in some more. I remember being a little puzzled as they all had the same kinds of titles.

I had never seen these little paperback books before, so I started reading one under the desk in the next class. I continued through geography, and history, and religious instruction. I read until dinner time and stuffed the book under my jumper during dinner, so I could read it as I walked back to the dormitory, where I read until lights out. Miss Mac was right. The little books certainly kept my mind off worrying! Although I noticed a secret smile the very next day when I asked her for more, it didn't occur to me until decades later that being unmarried and middle-aged maybe she lived vicariously through these books…

And so began an addiction to Mills and Boon romances which flared up intermittently until I was an adult. I loved reading them! I even shared the 'good ones' with my mum and sister, and every holiday season we would binge-read a box of them and then take them to the book exchange for replacements.

As I got older, I found that the boy meets girl, girl pretends not to like boy but goes for his arch rival, boy does something wonderful for girl and then she realises she loves him formula became less interesting with each story, but the settings of the books began to fascinate me more. Sometimes, I even skipped over the romantic bits to find out more quickly which town/village/island/planet the heroine was going to next. And that was how I first heard about Peninsula Valdes, in Argentina. Years before our field trip, I had read a Mills and Boon romance set on Peninsula Valdes, about a female marine biologist who was there studying whales. I have no recollection with whom she fell in love, but I remember being struck by the description of the location, and wondering if it was fiction or fact. I remember telling Peter, who periodically mocked my low-brow reading (even though I interspersed it with high-brow reading…really!) about the peninsula. He confirmed it as a very important breeding ground of Southern right whales. When we planned our field trip to South America, he agreed that it was a place we should visit.

It was therefore a long held dream of mine come true when we drove towards Peninsula Valdes. The road passed through scrubby flats, where the sight of bushes festooned with windblown rubbish was the only sign of an upcoming village or town. The occasional windmill also broke the horizon in this seemingly desolate and windy land, although we did see large emu-like rheas now and again. In the late afternoon, we entered the peninsula, and as dusk fell we were still driving towards the camping area by the beach. As we set up in the dark, Lucho must have detected my disappointment that we had not arrived earlier to see the whales, and he assured me that the moment I looked outside in the morning, the first thing I would see would be a whale. He was right. In fact, when we woke up the next morning it was to the sound of a whale expelling air from its blowhole. I could barely contain my joy.

When we looked out of the window to the glassy sea, we spotted a mother whale and calf about eighty metres from the shore. They were just delightful – tails and heads whooshing up in the water, mirroring each other in exactly the same way I would play with my babies in a few years! It was a lovely way to start the day, which was just as well, as overall I recall being somewhat disappointed in the peninsula. I had expected to see an abundance of seals and guanacos and maras, but the wildlife was scanty. The reasons became clear when we learnt that the whole peninsula was owned by farmers, that camping was only permitted at two places, and that walking onto the beaches was forbidden. While the coastline was attractive, it was not spectacular, and the vegetation was identical to thousands of kilometres of pampas we had already crossed. Of even more importance was that there was no fresh water, so we would need to use our bottled emergency water supplies. While I was keen to stay, Lucho, Checho and Pedro were not. Eventually, they agreed to another night there after I argued that we needed a break from the endless work of trapping, and the clean sea wind to blow away the weeks of pampas dust.

So we drove many long hours around the peninsula despite, from my perspective, little pay-off either scenically or in terms of whale watching, as we didn't see any more whales after the first morning. At every minor variation in vegetation, Lucho and Pedro would stop the *camionetta* to investigate the types of insects, while Peter and Checho hunted for lizards. I felt out of sorts as I had thought it was supposed to be a little holiday, but everyone kept on working. I spent time gazing at the sky and wallowing in self-pity about my state of personal hygiene.

Before the trip, I had never let my body go unwashed for more than a day or two, or my hair go unwashed for weeks. It was curious how my hair did not seem to get any dirtier after the first fortnight, almost as if it had reached some natural state of balance. When travelling, unless we found a river, our water was very limited, so we used only the scantiest amount to wash the dishes and all else was saved for drinking. I didn't mind too much being dirty when we saw no one else, but when we left the peninsula, we were heading back to the town of Puerto Madryn, which we had passed through briefly on our way to the peninsula in the midst of an arctically cold dust storm. We were to meet with some other scientists, including one well-known Argentinian, about whom Lucho had a very definite and somewhat scathing opinion.

As it turned out, in addition to being unwashed when I met the visiting scientists the next day in Puerto Madryn, we were all also exhausted. In the middle of the night in torrential rain, Lucho had woken everyone and made us strike camp. He was worried that the vehicles would get bogged in the unmade road near the beach. Finding a place to park on the side of the made road then also proved to be difficult, as there was vegetation right to the very edges of the road. By the time we found somewhere, it was nearly dawn and we only had an hour or two before we needed to be on our way. As soon as it was full daylight, we drove to a spot overlooking the town, so we could watch for whales. During breakfast, there was a huge bump at the back of the campervan. We all raced outside to see that the *camionetta*, which had been parked behind the campervan, had been blown into the campervan with the force of the wind! Fortunately, there was no real damage done, and we were able to hit the road to Puerto Madryn.

Cleaning up

Puerto Madryn is a picturesque seaside resort with a strong Welsh heritage halfway between Buenos Aires and Tierra del Fuego. When we arrived, the sky was blue, the sea was sparkling, and for the second day since we had arrived in Patagonia, there was no wind. Many shopfronts advertised what appeared to me to be familiar Australian surnames alongside Spanish or Gaelic words.

Peter had organised to meet up with a group of mammalogists from Buenos Aires. They were primarily keen to trap *tucu-tucus,* small burrowing rodents which are very similar to the prairie dogs of the USA. *Tucu-tucus* get their name from the noise they make, which apparently can be heard quite clearly from above ground as they move through their burrow systems. However, the mammalogists were also interested to hunt for the Patagonian opossum. Peter hoped that a larger team of trappers might have more success than our small crew.

I was both nervous and excited about meeting the mammalogists. On the one hand, they had organised some accommodation for Peter and me, a vehicle, and access to laboratory facilities at the Institute of Patagonian Studies. I was desperately hoping the accommodation might include a comfortable bed, and a clean bathroom with hot water. It would be interesting to meet some new people, even though none of them spoke English. The downside was that I was not sure how I would fit into the work of this new all-male team. I felt even more vulnerable when Lucho, Pedro and Checho left us in Puerto Madryn and hurriedly went away for a couple of days to trap insects. I wondered if that was Lucho's way of avoiding any interaction with the mammalogists. It made me reflect on the fact that, unlike most scientists, he did not hold a current position at any South American university, and I wondered if he was considered unconventional. Lucho took with him the travelling *monitos*, as we did not know whether we would be able to take proper care of them while working with the other team.

To my intense pleasure, and despite Peter's apprehension about whether it would be a good arrangement from the research perspective, all went well, mostly because their interest in the Patagonian opossum was a secondary concern. The first night, we were invited to dinner by the other five scientists to the flat where they were staying. I was hopeful of a home-cooked meal but was disappointed. We had a great deal of wine, a little bread, and by the time the *asado* finally arrived close to midnight, I was almost fainting from hunger. It made me realise how isolated we had been from regular life. Argentinians always eat late, but the activities of the field trip had been dictating our lifestyle for several weeks now. Even though I barely participated in the conversation, which was all in Spanish and zoological in nature, I enjoyed it. I had forgotten what it was like to have an evening like that.

On a positive note for me, it was clear that the mammalogists had not counted on me providing an extra pair of hands. Each day, Peter went with them to lay and check *tucu-tucu* traps in the sand dunes, and lay traps for the Patagonian opossum in an old quarry site. Relieved of my former duties, I spent literally hours in the shower, lathering and rinsing every part of me. I savoured every molecule of wetness, and relished in the joy of puckered skin as I walked around our private room wrapped in a clean, dry towel. I cut my broken and torn fingernails and toenails and was rewarded by seeing them look like my own hands and feet again. I scrubbed our clothes in hot water, and for the first time in very many weeks, was surprised to see myself in a mirror. Pleasingly, my skin was uncharacteristically tanned, but on closer inspection it was weather-beaten, chafed-looking and brown-wrinkled, not the healthy-looking brown-tanned I was expecting! I perceived myself to look, for the first time, every bit if not more of my thirty years. When I observed new white-etched worry lines on my forehead and around my eyes, I realised how tired I was, and I resolved to make the most of the next few days and concentrate on relaxing.

I walked along the beachfront promenade among the local inhabitants, admiring the beach, the pier, and the whitewashed holiday houses. To my great pleasure, on my first day in town, I saw more than ten whales lazing around in the bay about thirty to fifty metres from the beach, seemingly unconcerned by the windsurfers sailing around them. I could hardly believe that after hours of unsuccessfully scanning the horizon at the peninsula for whales, here they were so close. Fearing they would go away if I left to get some protection from the sun, I slowly burned while watching them. I saw mother whales rolling over on their backs in what appeared to be an action related to suckling their calves, and lots of tail slapping. The babies practised their breaching. Further out to sea, one larger whale, perhaps a male, entertained me and many others on the beachfront with a series of magnificent leaps, which resulted in spontaneous applause from the many passers-by. Later, I walked the length of the pier and saw a mother and baby swimming beside me and in and out of the boats which were tied up there.

Whales really are superb animals. I loved the four days we spent in Puerto Madryn. I remember Peter commenting that I seemed much more relaxed, and it was amazing what a good shower and bed, clean clothes, sunshine, whales, and an absence of pampas wind could achieve!

On the final day, Peter was asked to address the staff of the Instituto on reproduction in marsupials. I felt secretly proud both that he had been asked, and also that he felt able to give the talk in Spanish. Lucho collected me from the accommodation and we went to pick up Peter after his talk. As the staff spilled out of the Instituto, several of them were talking intently with Peter. As we watched and waited, Lucho commented quietly, 'Look at how important they think they all are!' This answered, I felt, my curiosity about his perception of himself in relation to that scientific community.

I have frequently remembered that comment of Lucho's throughout my academic career. Sometimes, it is possible to see, in a gathering of people with a common purpose, how the 'in-crowd' interact to both promote each other in an organisation and exclude others who might want to gain entry. Perhaps this is partly what is meant by the old boys' network. As a female non-clinician working in a medical faculty, I have often served on committees where both women and non-clinicians are in the minority. I am used to my opinions being trivialised or dismissed, although that happened less frequently once I was promoted to professor. Now, instead, I note the invisibility of being an older woman. Self-importance can be readily observed when watching a cluster of teenagers demanding attention in a store, or in the seemingly petty patronising instructions given out by those managing queues going through Customs. Feeling important seems to be more important than actually being important in our modern world.

The next morning, we arose early and left Puerto Madryn far behind. Even though I was sorry to leave behind the washing facilities, I was pleased to be away from the noise and activity of the town; quite some realisation for a born and bred city girl! It was clear from everyone's mood that we all felt elated to be back together. With our travelling *monitos*, we were like a little family, and I realised how much Lucho, Pedro and Checho had come to mean to me. For the first time, it occurred to me that perhaps they had missed me when Peter and I were staying in the accommodation, and that I had come to mean something to them too, although what that something was, I had no idea.

We drove along the coastal road to Punta Tombes. Along the road, eagle-eyed Checho spotted a skunk and we pulled over to watch it. Peter, never having seen a skunk up close, was keen to catch it. As everyone was chasing it, I felt sorry for the poor animal, and I ran after them remonstrating. But the skunk really didn't need my help, as it ran beneath a bush and sprayed us! Amusingly, for the others, only Peter and I got hit. The liquid apparently contains the same chemical compound that is present in rotting flesh, and certainly smelt disgusting. Our tainted clothes needed containment in a tightly closed plastic bag until the next river. Luckily, Peter and I had freshly laundered clothes to change into, thanks to the Instituto's accommodation in Puerto Madryn.

The pretty coastal road also passed through lots of open grassy areas which were the playground of thousands of different-coloured grasshoppers. Soon, we turned off to Cabo dos Bahias, where there was an enormous rookery of Magellanic penguins. We arrived as dusk fell. We watched the penguins trudge determinedly back to their nests after the day's fishing, amid a cacophony of welcomes from their partners. How they found their own nest in that enormous rookery was a mystery. The smell of salt and birds was overpowering. Around us on the hills we could see many guanacos in silhouette against the sunset and we could hear their curious whining vocalisation above the cries of seabirds.

We set up camp, laid the traps as usual, and Lucho set up his special insect-attracting light which cast long bluish shadows over the surrounding bushes to collect insects for the *monitos*. In the eleven p.m. trapline inspection, in addition to mice, we had caught a *cuis*, a rodent related to the guinea pig. He was almost the size of the trap, and so when we pulled him out, his fur retained the shape made by him pushing up against the corners of the trap. Many years later, I remembered this *cuis* when our younger daughter, who had masses of extremely curly hair, pushed herself into the corner of her cot and ended up with square hair.

After processing the *cuis* and the other mice we caught in the night-time check, we all went to bed. In the morning, when we woke up, one of our precious travelling *monitos*, Gabriella, was dead.

Pico Salamanca

We had been keeping detailed field notes on the travelling *monitos*. When we began to travel, initially we kept Gabriella separated from the others as she had been brought in by a different local Indian man. She had weighed twenty-three grams, and was the lightest, apart from Carlito, who at twenty-two grams appeared to be a juvenile male. Females Carolina and Caballero (who we initially believed to be male) and the mature male Mauricio weighed twenty-nine grams, twenty-nine grams and twenty-eight grams respectively when we left Chile. After a week or so of carefully observing behaviour to make sure they were all getting along together, we introduced Gabriella to the larger cage so she would not be lonely by herself.

Within a fortnight, the two males Carlito and Mauricio had gained two grams and five grams of weight respectively, and the dark pigmentation around Mauricio's scrotum was becoming much more obvious, suggesting that breeding season was soon to come. Female Caballero initially gained weight, but the other two females lost weight; Carolina had lost five grams and Gabriella four grams. We observed the *monitos* a lot to make sure that none of them were missing out on food or being threatened by the others. With little other information on *monitos* in captivity, it was impossible to know whether the weight loss was significant, but I recall Peter saying that since Gabriella and Carolina had both lost the same percentage of body weight, maybe it was what happened to females prior to the breeding season.

Peter performed an autopsy on Gabriella, and although he noted her stomach was empty at the time of her death, in all other ways she seemed quite healthy. It was impossible to tell if she had been ill or succumbed to an infection the others might have had when brought in.

We had also observed that inside the nest at night sometimes was a scratching or beating sound at high intensity, a bit like a dog scratching at a flea. It was a reminder that there were likely to be travelling microorganisms such as lice and ticks travelling on our travelling *monitos*, and the effect of them on the health of the animals was unknown.

Gabriella's death dampened everyone's spirits, but there was still work to be done. We packed up camp and headed south. Our ultimate destination was Pico Salamanca, where there was a record of one male and three female Patagonian opossums having been caught in the 1920s (Simpson, 1972). Unfortunately, the paper in which it was reported did not specify whether the animals had been caught on the actual peak (*pico*), the Estancia Pico Salamanca, or simply the region of Pico Salamanca, which encompasses quite a few estancias. To get to any of those places, though, we needed to go through to Comodora Rividavia.

On our way south, we trapped at Estancia La Cantera. We camped in the dry rocky bottom of an enormous gully known in Spanish as a *quebrada*. The steep slopes were topped with rocky outcrops streaked with guano, suggesting it was a popular place for birds. Over three nights we trapped, and we caught tens of mice. In the little free time we had, we would climb to the top of the slopes to search for owl pellets just outside the many caves. This was treacherous work as there was nothing to cling on to going up and down the dry, sandy slopes, and it was difficult to maintain balance while bending or squatting to collect the owl pellets. Among the rubble of the owl pellets, we were surprised to find a very old human skull with the teeth intact. We left it there, exactly where we found it, and moved along to another cave. We had no wish to disturb a burial ground.

On the day we decided to move on, we were all packed up ready to go when we realised that Checho was missing. Lucho blasted the horn of the *camionetta*, and it reverberated loudly up and down the valley. Lucho continued to blast the horn every few minutes over a period of fifteen minutes or more, as we became increasingly agitated about Checho. Where could he be? There was no way he could not hear the horn.

I was worried that he was lying unconscious somewhere, or had fallen and broken his leg. Lucho seemed to be angry, as if he expected that Checho was deliberately ignoring him.

In the end, that appeared to be true. Peter, Pedro and I walked quite a distance up the valley and eventually spotted Checho high on a rocky outcrop. He had discovered an enormous mound of owl pellets, the biggest we had ever seen, and was busy collecting them into bags. This find was to keep us even busier in the coming weeks than we had ever been, and proved to be the source of several jawbones and other small bones from the Patagonian opossum. Little did I know that the loss of those bones, alongside the diaries, would be a topic of interest for me still thirty years later!

The view from the road on the way to Comodora Rivadavia in dry and dusty southern Argentina was peppered with dozens of little drill heads bobbing up and down as they pumped oil to the surface. Small satellite towns, like Astra, bore the names of petrol brands. As we came into the outskirts of Comodora Rivadavia, we could see the distinctive orange and black oil pumps even between houses and fenced off in children's playgrounds. There was very little vegetation, only low well-spaced prickle bushes and shrubs. There was not a tree to be seen anywhere in the distant hills, although we saw several eucalypt trees dotting the yards of houses. It was the first town we had visited for ages, and after Lucho dropped us off so we could run some errands, I recall Peter and I feeling odd and disconnected from the other shoppers. We wondered if it was that the only two towns we had visited in the previous few weeks had been holiday resorts, rather than business centres. We also noticed people here had very different expectations of customers. At one place, it took an hour and the partaking of coffee insistently offered by the proprietor to successfully make a simple money transaction, and at another we had to engage in thirty minutes of conversation before we could get some photos developed. There seemed to be some expectation that you would want to know each other before you would agree to commence the business transaction. It was different to anything we had previously experienced.

Everything in Argentina stopped from one to three thirty p.m., so we had time to kill during siesta. As we strolled in the sun by the pleasant, if windy, pebble beach which faced the wharves, several noisy fighter planes flew overhead, reminding us that Argentina had lost the battle for the Falklands Islands in a ten-week-long war only three years previously. It made us wonder whether the lengthy business transactions we had experienced were somehow related to misperceptions that we were British, and therefore untrustworthy.

We walked further along to the beach just south of the city, where there were dozens of green and brown lizards hiding amongst the low bushes on the sand dunes. Lucho hunted for beetles, and Pedro and Peter enjoyed a swim. Once again, being female dictated my activity. I walked for miles along the beach in search of a place that might offer me some privacy. I was menstruating and needed to change my tampon and safely bury the used one. As I left, I felt resentful that no one even asked where I was going, or if I was okay, and when I returned over ninety minutes later, it seemed that no one had even noted my absence, compounding my menstrual grumpiness.

The next day as we drove through the coastal areas south of Comodoro Rivadavia, we stopped frequently to check for insects. We were amazed to see oil seeping up through our footprints as we walked over some spongy ground. This would not have been surprising closer to Comodora, but we had travelled almost two days since then. It made me wonder about the size of the untapped oilfields, and how far south they might extend.

Late one afternoon, we pulled into the Estancia de los Rosas to ask for directions to Pico Salamanca. We drove past several run-down buildings, including a shearing shed. There were a number of gauchos of varying shapes and sizes at work in the yard. As we drove in, they stared. For the first time anywhere in the trip, no one offered a greeting of any kind. Clearly we were not welcome visitors. Checho got out of the vehicle and asked one man if he knew the way to Pico Salamanca. He could offer no advice.

As it was getting late, and the estancia had a well, Lucho asked if we could camp there for the night. There were seven or eight gauchos, and the way they looked at me made me scared – it was the only time in the trip where I felt seriously uncomfortable. It was likely that none of them had ever seen a female travelling with several men in such a way – they probably wondered what on earth my role was amongst these men. I stayed inside the van the whole time we were there and only ventured out to go to the toilet in a nearby field. For this, Peter and I walked a long way away from the buildings – and even then I felt scared. I lay awake most of the night while the others slept – feeling as if I needed to be on guard, not just for me, but for us all.

As dawn rose, I heard many sets of horses' hooves clopping past the campervan, and when I peeped out of the window I saw all of the gauchos heading off over the pampas, each wearing a look of grim determination. As they left, it occurred to me that perhaps I had mistaken their facial expressions as menacing, when in fact they were anxious about their own work, or even what we might want of them or to do to them. It hammered home to me how much of life swings on good communication, and how easily we default to the least positive explanation when we don't understand each other. Many years later, the lesson was repeated when I once again made a totally unfounded assumption.

We were visiting our colleague and friend Tom in Sydney, and had taken Daughter One, who was just a toddler, to the local park to play. There was another little girl there, of about four or five, who I thought must belong to the family who were a long way away, seated at the picnic tables. She had taken off her jumper and was busy running around. I was pushing my daughter on the swing when I suddenly noticed a creepy-looking young man emerge from the nearby male toilets. He picked up the little girl's jumper and sat down near her holding it. He looked furtively about. I couldn't take my eyes off him, I was sure he was going to use the jumper to start a conversation with the child and maybe entice her away from the playground. I was so concerned I pointed it out to Tom and we both stood and watched them.

Suddenly the little girl ran over to the man and said, 'Come on, Dad, let's go!'

So not a paedophile, but her own father! Yet another case of my overactive imagination serving me badly...

After a lot of indecisive map-reading and several disappointing failures we finally found a road to the peak named Pico Salamanca, which, it transpired, was on private property, and the track leading in was blocked by a padlocked gate. It was now November, and it was the hottest, clearest weather we had experienced. We had a wonderful view of a crystal-clear sea, but no access to it. We were stuck high on the mountain, amongst armpit-high prickle bushes. We were, however, all keen to see whether there were any live Patagonian opossums, so we decided to lay traps there, off a track away from the road, near the entrance to Pico Salamanca. Lucho and Pedro decided to set up camp near whatever water they could find, leaving Checho and Peter and me to lay the traps. Despite the use of machetes, it was incredibly difficult to carry, lay and check the traps, and we wore the many scars for months afterwards. It was impossible not to be frustrated about the trapping conditions, and we were all somewhat short with each other. To make it worse, we had no drinking water and were hot and thirsty and dusty and had multiple scratches and scrapes.

Lucho and Pedro had searched while we set the traps but had been unable to find water anywhere. So they had set up camp near a rusty animal trough filled by water pumped up by a windmill. Remembering my earlier experience with an animal trough, I privately vowed I would never use it. But by the second day of blistering heat, and faced with diminishing water supplies, I had to change my mind. I knew I could not physically navigate through kilometres of prickle bushes to try to find a creek and then clamber back up carrying water, so I just turned my head away when I came upon Lucho scraping away brown sediment and algae from the bottom of the trough with a soup ladle.

Of course we ended up being grateful for the trough water not only for washing dishes and ourselves, but for boiling before using in cooking. Again I admonished myself for having to suppress feelings of revulsion when I thought of the cattle drool, and rust, and waterborne insects which I was swallowing with every mouthful, even if they were dead or denatured. I really should have toughened up by now. After all, every day, work continued on the campervan table. Dead mice were skinned there, insects and owl pellets were dissected, and while the blood or tissue was wiped away last thing at night, often lunch was served amongst the gore. Why couldn't I just put thoughts about cleanliness out of my mind?

After a few days of heavy trapping (the trapping notes state 'there is an incredible biomass of mice at Pico Salamanca') but with no success at all at finding Patagonian opossums, we all felt exhausted and decided to drive into a few other estancias on the way to our next stop, to ask if they had heard or seen any Patagonian opossums. It was fascinating to see the different types of homesteads. Some were accessed from an avenue of well-established English trees and manicured lawns, and others were very humble cement or mudbrick dwellings. One of the locals explained that the big old estancias were owned by those with English, Scottish or Welsh backgrounds, and the adobe ones were built by Spaniards. Apparently, there was even a community of Boers near Pico Salamanca, who arrived just after the Boer War. We went to several estancias, but no one had ever heard of the animals. Feeling a little downhearted, we decided to move further south towards Cabo Tres Puntas.

La Madrugada

Although the first ever Patagonian opossum was recorded to have been caught in a fox trap at 'Estancia Madujada, not far from Puerto Deseado' (Thomas, 1929: 45), we could find no evidence of such an estancia. Having looked long and hard at the available maps, and asked the very few local people we passed, the closest name we could find (remember, it was pre Google map days!) was La Madrugada. So we decided to give it a try.

We had no trouble finding the estancia. Several men were busy moving sheep around in the yard, and they told us the owner was out. A man appeared at the entrance to the shearing shed and invited us in. Once inside, we could see several men shearing sheep using electric clippers of a style that was common in Australia in the 1930s. He then invited us into their kitchen for maté. It was immediately obvious to me from the calendars featuring topless women on the wall that this kitchen was used exclusively by men. No sooner had we sat down on a bench and begun the sharing of the maté, than the very young and good-looking estancia owner arrived.

When he heard about our search for the Patagonian opossum, Juan-Lucas was most welcoming. He said he lived alone there, although he clearly had several male workers who lived with him on the estancia. His parents owned a fashion house in Buenos Aires and spoke to their son twice a day on a ham radio.

Juan-Lucas spoke perfect English, as well as Italian and Spanish, the languages of his grandparents. He was an excellent conversationalist and over the next few days we learnt a lot from him about politics and education and the Argentinian economy. He had attended university and was keen to discuss the possibility of artificial insemination for his sheep, so he was very pleased to be able to discuss it with Peter, whose specialty was reproduction. At that time, artificial insemination had only been used in cattle in Argentina.

Best of all, he offered us a camping place on his private beach, which was completely untouched. The beach was made of different sizes of multicoloured pebbles, mostly worn smooth. At one end was a *loberia* or seal colony, and nearby was a cormorant nesting colony. It was very picturesque, although, being so close to so many animals, very smelly. However, the chance to be close to the water, and the absence of prickles on the bushes made the prospect of staying there very appealing.

The first evening, while Lucho, Pedro and Checho were out laying insect traps, Peter and I sat on the beach about twenty metres away from the seals. They were clearly quite interested in us, turning to gauge our reaction to various activities that were taking place amongst their group, and watching the interactions between Peter and me. They were really most engaging, and I did not feel the least bit threatened. It was a hot evening and when Peter suggested a dip, I agreed. What I hadn't expected was that the seals would also take up his offer, and within a minute or two they had joined us.

They swam alongside us with their heads popping up every now and again to see what we were doing. It was an amazing experience, swimming with twenty seals. Being at such close quarters allowed us to discriminate slight differences between them, both in appearance and behaviour, and I could fully understand the attraction of getting to know these good-natured mammals. After fifteen minutes or so of playing in the water, I was getting very cold and decided to finish my swim. To my surprise, Peter followed me. When I remarked that I thought he might have wanted to have stayed in longer, he said he hadn't wanted to frighten me while we were in the water, but he knew that orcas and sharks were often found near seal colonies.

I was firstly surprised and then upset with him that he hadn't told me. But I quickly recognised that had I known that, I would have declined the opportunity and missed out on an amazing experience. In retrospect, I wonder whether such a situation – finding out about potential danger after the event – might have contributed to the stress of living with Peter. His ability to ignore any potentially negative outcomes meant I always felt compelled to worry for two.

Camping on our own private beach had many positives, but in the middle of the night, I found a negative. There was only one narrow dirt road that ran towards the beach, and then the last kilometre or so we had just navigated through the vegetation to park just next to where the pebble beach became solid ground. I had gone to sleep with the windows of the campervan open to enjoy the soothing sound of the waves. But at about two a.m., it sounded as if the waves were seriously about to engulf us. I leapt out of bed. It was a bright moonlit night, and the waves were indeed a lot closer. I woke Peter, who went outside and watched the waves for a few minutes.

He came back inside saying he thought it would be fine, and it was probably only a spring tide, and I should go back to sleep. A spring tide? What was that? He explained that spring tides occur when the moon is either new or full, and the sun, the moon and the earth are aligned, and it was then that the biggest difference between high and low tide is seen. He could not see any signs of a high-water mark on the beach but assumed that, since we were parked amongst vegetation, the sea would not come this high. Still I felt uneasy. I remember watching the sea until dawn. It was only when I heard Checho getting up and moving around outside that I felt safe enough to go to sleep.

We were very busy at La Madrugada. We needed to catch insects each day to feed the travelling *monitos*, and keep their cage clean. We trapped literally hundreds of mice, which were all identified and released. While laying or checking traps, we had also found several Indian middens, and many flechas or arrowheads. One day when we were clambering over rocks, I spotted a pile of extremely old bones in a crevice, which, on closer inspection, turned out to be human. Juan-Lucas was very excited by the discovery and was keen for us to take the bones away to have their age determined. I felt uncomfortable about removing them from their resting place, and Peter was concerned about the complexities of international travel with human remains, but eventually agreed to take the axis and atlas, the topmost vertebrae of the spine, to see if he could get the age determined.

Although Juan-Lucas could not have been more supportive of our endeavours, we found no evidence at all of the Patagonian opossum. Over the course of the few days we stayed there, Juan-Lucas visited us a few times for a chat. He came down one evening bringing a leg of lamb, and some lettuce and radishes, the first fresh vegies we had had for weeks. Despite his enthusiasm and kindness, we eventually decided it was time to move on. Peter had organised for one of his PhD students, David, to fly into Coyhaique, in Chile, to assist us with more *monito* work, and we needed to be there to collect him.

Mauricio exposed

Even though we were having no luck on the Patagonian opossum hunt, the travelling *monitos* were very easy to maintain in captivity. As our journey through Argentina had progressed, the two males began to show quite noticeable increases in testicular size, suggesting that they were coming into breeding condition. Towards the end of November, the travelling *monitos* all seemed to lose some condition, and so additional protein was added to their diet – more grasshoppers and moths. We had put two old nests we had found in the Chilean forest into their cage, and they all took up residence there. Following the introduction of moths to their diet, Caballero was observed making a new nest near the feeding hole. Clever Caballero!

Interestingly, the new nest-building occurred not long after Mauricio had had surgery to remove one of his testicles. This, after all, was one of the reasons Peter had come to South America, to learn about the size, shape and composition of the sperm of *monito*. Acquiring a sample of sperm is not always as easy in animals as it can be in humans. Rabbits, for example, can be easily trained to ejaculate into an artificial vagina carefully held by a human just beneath the entry to the vagina of a teaser female rabbit astride the human's arm. In zoos, if animals are endangered species and have failed to reproduce naturally, sometimes the animal is anaesthetised and a small electric shock is delivered near to the prostate using a rectal probe to cause an ejaculation of semen which can be collected to inseminate females artificially.

None of this was possible for the tiny *monitos*, and Peter did not want any of them to have to be sacrificed for science unnecessarily. He had been checking the males regularly to see whether there was any sperm present in the urine. This was no mean feat and required close observation (often by me) of the animals to determine the activity signs which suggested a wee was imminent, and then quickly getting a pipette to extract the drop of fluid from wherever it had fallen. Once sperm started appearing in the urine of Mauricio, Peter, with the assistance of a very proud but nervous Pedro, operated on him under anaesthetic to remove just one testicle. If Peter had misjudged Mauricio's reproductive status, leaving one testicle would offer a second bite at the cherry, so to speak.

Performing the operation was actually quite risky, as there are no guidelines on how much anaesthetic would be enough to control the pain but allow Mauricio a good recovery. It was essential to sterilise all the instruments and to ensure that Mauricio did not get an infection post-operatively, by licking his wound or exposing it to some pathogen. Peter had had a lot of experience with animal surgery in the laboratory, and so was reasonably confident all would go well. But I was still a little apprehensive for several days, until it was clear that Mauricio had made an excellent recovery and was able to be put back with the other *monitos*.

Mauricio's reproductive tract yielded information which appeared to support Peter's hypothesis (Temple-Smith 1987). Unlike Max's sperm, and that of all other South American marsupials which had yet been tested, the sperm in Mauricio's reproductive tract had not formed pairs in the epididymis. The unpaired sperm were similar to the single sperm in Australian marsupials, offering evidence of a close relationship between the animals and suggesting a common evolutionary ancestor. But there was a catch. Mauricio's sperm was not paired, but it was also only poorly motile, suggesting that he was not really in the midst of the breeding cycle or that his reproductive maturity might have been affected by the travel conditions and his diet, which, while adequate, had included insects found in Argentina rather than Chile.

Even without obtaining more sperm from other males to strengthen the evidence, Mauricio's testicle was a treasure chest which became the focus of an article in a scientific journal. However, more males, in peak breeding condition under natural conditions, were now needed to confirm our observations.

Back to Chile

Periodically, we had vehicle problems. Such situations made our isolation from civilisation all the more tangible. Lucho was always positive that Checho could fix whatever the problem might be, so Checho would duly spend an hour or so under the bonnet of the vehicle before announcing that to repair it would need equipment you could only find at a mechanic's. Given the distances and terrain over which we were travelling, it seems short-sighted in retrospect that we had not planned to have regular services booked in en route, but it was pre-mobile phone and pre-internet days and it would have been impossible to have planned such a thing in advance. So when Checho announced he could not fix whatever was wrong, which was often the case, typically Lucho would then be optimistic that the problem might resolve itself, and if that was not the case by the next town we went through, we would stop to visit a mechanic.

After leaving La Madrugada, the road towards Chile took us through Lago Blanco, where, despite our doubts judging from the deserted streets, we were able to find a mechanic. While he looked at the van, Peter and I wandered over to Hosteria Las Flores, which strangely was both a pub and a grocery store. We drank coffee and chatted to a little boy whose parents owned the hotel. He had an enormous smile, and was earnestly interested in Peter's by now very large beard. He asked Peter many questions, such as what would he do if someone attacked him by grabbing it? He enthusiastically demonstrated some creative karate moves which Peter might execute if such a situation arose. He was such a delightful personality that I subsequently wrote to my family and asked them to send him a little memento of Australia, since we had nothing with us to give him. This interaction very pleasantly passed the time until the mechanic reported back the good news that all the campervan needed was a new brake cable. The bad news was that the closest supply of the cable was five hundred kilometres away, in Chile. He managed to patch together enough cable to make the brakes effective on one wheel, and urged us to go directly to Coyhaique to get the brakes fixed properly.

We crossed the border back into Chile at the start of December. We left behind the wide open pampas and the sparsely vegetated hills in Argentina, and began to encounter more trees and undergrowth with increasing foliage as the air became damper on the western side of the Andes. Driving in the campervan had become a little scary, but so far we had been managing.

Whenever we went downhill near other vehicles, bridges or where there might be people, though, everyone jumped out of the van and walked ahead to make sure the road was clear. This rather slowed our progress and there was some anxiety, I recall, that we would not make it to Coyhaique in time to collect David, Peter's PhD student, from the airport. In most places in the world this would not be a problem, and uncollected passengers could fend for themselves. However, there the airport was forty kilometres from the town, there was no public transport and only one flight per day. So it was likely that once passengers had been collected, the airport would be closed until tomorrow's flight. David spoke no Spanish, and there were no mobile telephones in those days. So there was quite a bit of pressure to get there promptly.

Eventually, the *camionetta* was dispatched as an advance party with Peter and Lucho on board, and Checho, Pedro and I were left to manage the campervan. It was quite nerve-racking, but some hours later we met up with the others with David at a fork in the road and proceeded carefully to the night's campsite.

After two weeks without a wash, Lucho had promised me we would stay in a camping ground or beside a good river for one night so we could have a really good clean-up. I had been menstruating; I was looking forward to washing my hair and shaving my underarms, so I was bitterly disappointed when he parked next to a river which flowed through an open plain with no vegetation other than tufty grass.

Although the water did not look too dirty, the abundance of animal footprints suggested walking barefoot by the river might result in more than just sand between the toes. We arrived just before sunset, at around nine p.m., and the men all dived in and washed and shampooed their hair. They chatted loudly, clearly enjoying washing away the grime and sweat of the last few weeks.

I stood for a long time at the water's edge. No one even glanced my way. No one asked if I was joining them or if I was OK; they just continued to talk and laugh. Eventually, I walked downstream a bit to try to find a private place to wash. The wind was picking up, there was no warmth in the last rays of the setting sun, and there was no privacy anywhere. I did not want to wash alone in the dark. Yet if I did not wash then, in that freezing water, there might not be another chance for weeks! Eventually, as night fell, I washed myself limb by limb, crying all the time and wishing that Peter had chosen to wash with me rather than the men. Sometimes, I didn't want to be one of the boys. I wanted to be special, and I wanted my husband to notice that some things were just harder for me.

However, I did feel special later when David unpacked his daypack and handed me a fat bundle of letters from home. There were letters from all of my workmates, and letters from all the family as well as two very welcome gifts from my mum – a tube of traveller's washing detergent and a jar of Vegemite. It was such a relief to hear that all was well with everyone at home. I had not realised how much tension I was holding in, as it had been over two months since we had left home and the last time we had managed to make a call was before we had left Chile to go to Argentina. David had actually been to see my family before he had come away, and that made his report even better. Peter's family lived in Tasmania, but my family had been in regular contact with them, so David was able to tell us their news too. And of course he also had brought some scientific supplies we needed.

Two days later, an additional person arrived whom I had never previously met: a senior scientist from the Zoology Department at Monash University. Tony had a special interest in small mammals, especially small carnivorous marsupials, and was happy to make a financial contribution to the field trip to be able to trap alongside us. So our small team of four men and one woman became six men and one woman. I wondered what it might mean for the group.

Above: Institute of Zoology, London. We had left the bags just inside the door to the right.

Left: The temperate forest at Puyehue National Park, dominated by *Nothofagus dombeyi*.

Above: An Elliot trap and an Akodon. Note the grains of oats used to encourage the rat to leave the trap for this photo. In the wet Chilean rainforest each trap was inserted into a plastic freezer bag, to offer some protection to the trapped animal.

Below: *Dromiciops gliroides*, commonly known as 'Monito del Monte'.

Above: Monitos in torpor.

Left: A monito nest.

Left: The forest near Lago Chapo, before clearing, showing the commonly seen secondary growth bamboo thickets in the foreground.

Below: The forest near Lago Chapo, during clearing. It shows the stump from which the woodcutters caught Max (*Rhyncolestes raphanurus*).

Above: Post-bathing in a rocky river near Puyehue.

Below: Los Manantiales, Argentina: The ancient river bed is surrounded by high cliffs with many caves. This is where we searched for owl pellets.

Left: Los Manantiales. The view from the other side of the riverbed. Lucho and Pedro searching for insects on the eroded slope leading to the cliff face.

Below: Semi-arid scrubland plateau of Argentinian Patagonia showing the size of the ancient river beds with the snowcapped Andes in the distance.

Above: Bathing in the Chubut River, showing the van and the camionetta.

Below: Lucho, post-bath in the Chubut River.

Above: Occasionally in Patagonia, we passed other traffic.

Below: It was always interesting to see others in the vast landscape – almost everyone was on horseback.

Above: Lucho photographing sea lions at the penguin rookery at Cabos dos Bahias, Argentina. Note the pebble beaches typical of some of the eastern coastline of Argentina.

Below: The stock trough at Pico Salamanca, Argentina, which provided our drinking water.

Above: Los Madrugada, Argentina: about to swim with the seals.

Below: Chilean Patagonia – on the way to Coyhaique.

Left and below: Crossing river using the ferry. There were almost no bridges this far south.

Above: Peter in a forest of nalca or Chilean rhubarb plants (*Gunnera tinctoria*). We used the leaves of these plants as umbrellas, and they were also used in cooking the curanto at Lago Chapo.

Below: Wooden church on Chiloe Island.

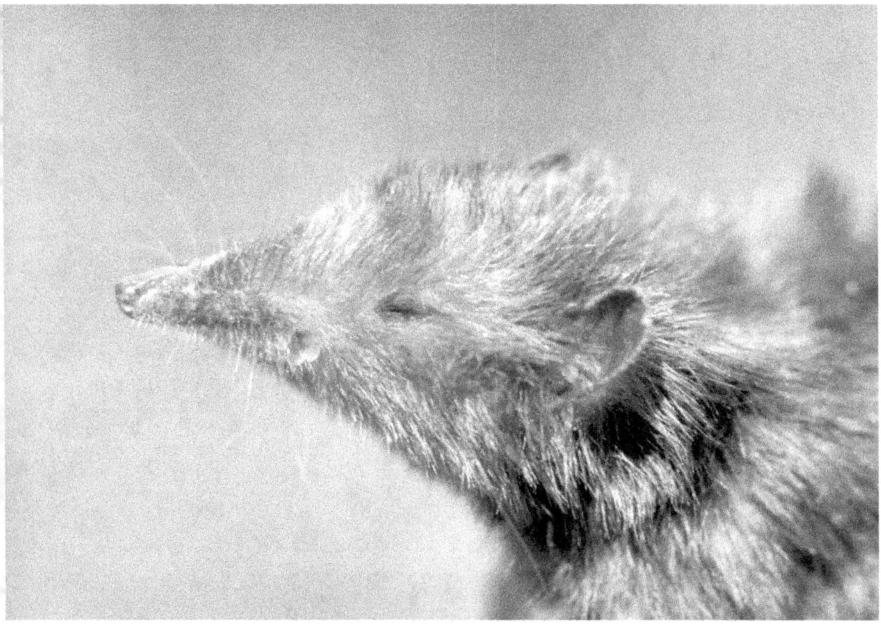

Above: Maxine (*Rhyncolestes raphanurus*).
Caught on Chiloe Island, she later featured in a wildlife documentary.

Below: Peter bathing in the Cucao River, Chiloe Island.
I wanted to join him but felt too visible.

The curanto on Christmas Day, Lago Chapo. The seafood, meat and vegetables were cooked beneath the nalca leaves, which were then covered in turf.

Above: The nalca leaves.

Left: The food.

Above: Doing the washing on Chiloe Island.

Below: On our way up to the area where we ran down the volcanic ash slopes. Vulcan Osorno is near the lake in the background.

Above: Taking field measurements during small mammal trapping.

Below: Picturesque Chile.

Five become seven

With the arrival of the two Australians, relationships changed, and I found to my surprise that I became a pivotal point in interactions between the Aussies and the Chilenos. There were some (virtual) scramblings and jostlings for positions within the team. Although it was good to have two extra pairs of hands, there were also more people to please, and more stomachs and egos to be fed. I found I was consulted a lot about the availability and use of supplies, and a measure of my improvement in Spanish was that I was often asked to translate Spanish into English for the two Aussies who spoke no Spanish.

This situation was a great contrast to how the team operated with five: then Peter was the boss, and Lucho was the orchestrator who decided when we would move and where, and when we would go near a town for supplies. Despite Lucho's initial lack of enthusiasm for a woman's presence on the trip, I know that in the end he respected me, because he even suggested he would name a new species of beetle after me.

Checho was more energetic and physically capable than Lucho, and very experienced in fieldwork, and so was Peter's right-hand man. Checho treated me with respect, and also watched out for me at times when I might have expected my husband to do so, such as clambering up a mountain carrying heavy traps, or wading through a river. He also was puzzled at the differences between me and the Chileno women he knew. He could not believe that I had reached the age of thirty and had no children. I think that he had not met any women who had a career, and certainly had not met many, if any, who travelled with men on a field trip like ours.

Pedro, in contrast, had started the trip calling us Don Peter and

Señora Meredith until I had asked him not to. He was a very modest young man; with our shared sleeping arrangements in Puyehue, I had observed that he undressed in his sleeping bag, and read his Bible every night. He also jumped up to anticipate my needs, and was the first to offer me a log to sit on, or a cup of tea. I noticed he sometimes looked at me to seek my intervention when Lucho or Checho suggested something which he wasn't keen to do, and after my Spanish improved, I was not surprised to learn that this was his first trip away from home.

We now have a son in his early twenties, around the same age as Pedro was when he went off on our trip; I can imagine it would have been a comfort to him have a woman in the group. So we had managed to find some ease in our relationships, and with the arrival of the two new male Aussies, one a professor of about Lucho's age, and one a young PhD student, all the relationship balls were thrown up into the air.

Tony was senior academically to Peter, although would not have come to South America if Peter had not organised it. David was Peter's student, and thus his junior, but they had worked closely for some time and I had known David for many years. I could imagine that Checho might feel usurped.

Completely inadvertently, I made this relationship between Checho and David much harder than it needed to be.

Peter has long been someone who falls to sleep in awkward places and at inconvenient times. Among his work colleagues and students, such stories had become legendary, and frequently people vied with each other to tell the most outrageous story of Peter's inappropriate shut-eye.

One of his former students swears, for example, that at a dinner in a Chinese restaurant to celebrate the handing in of her thesis, Peter nodded off over the soup, and his beard ended up in the soup festooned with spring onions. Peter himself tells a story of once when he was teaching a class after driving all night returning from a wombat field trip, he turned to draw something on the blackboard and felt himself drop off to sleep standing up. When eventually he turned round, the class was staring at him intently, with puzzled looks, until eventually someone asked if he was OK.

His dropping off to sleep during events with family and friends was indulgently excused on the basis of long hours of work, but some years later was found to be caused by sleep apnoea. However, I found the snoring to be way more frustrating than the sleeping. The volume of Peter's snoring was epic, and many of his students who had experienced his snoring on student camps suggested he pitch his tent a half a kilometre away from camp on subsequent trips.

For me, the snoring was a really big problem, as I frequently was unable to sleep through it. We started every night at home in the same bed, but once my prodding and poking and pushing him onto his side failed, and the snoring reached pneumatic drill volume, I moved to the spare room. That was tricky on the field trip. The longer the trip went on, the more important sleep became to us all. Our diet diminished in quality as we travelled further and further away from towns, and we felt run-down. We often kept very long hours with trapping, collecting and processing animals, as it is important to get them back to the wild as quickly as possible.

Until this point in the trip, Peter and I had sometimes shared the campervan bed, but he also pitched his two-man tent nearby so that if anyone was working on the table in the campervan and either or both of us wanted to sleep, we had somewhere to go; well, that was the party line at the start. In fact, we often ended up sleeping separately because of the snoring. Lucho always slept in the *camionetta*, and Pedro and Checho would sleep rolled up in sleeping bags by the campfire. Later in the trip, because of the wind and the cold, sometimes Pedro and Checho would fall asleep inside the van on the benches beside the table where they had been working, while I slept over the driver's cabin.

The night that Tony arrived, we had a welcome dinner. We had fresh food supplies as we had been successful in catching some trout, and as I recall, we each had a couple of the delicious South American aperitif, pisco sour, to celebrate our expanded field team.

We all turned in at the same time; the three Chilenos sleeping on the ground by the fire and in the *camionetta*, Tony in a one-man tent, and David in Peter's tent. In the night, Peter's relentless and possibly alcohol-fuelled snoring drove me crazy and I got out of bed, and went to Peter's tent, now occupied by David. I asked him if it was OK if I slept there, and he, also with vast prior experience of Peter's snoring, sleepily said, 'No worries.'

In the morning, as I climbed out of the tent, I was met by a bemused look from Lucho and Tony, a shocked look from Pedro, and an absolutely horrified look from Checho. I tried to explain to Checho that it had been an innocent sleeping emergency, but he was positively contemptuous, and said, in Spanish of course, that he could not believe I would make such a fool of Don Peter, my husband. I explained that David was married (in fact only for a month, at that stage!) and Peter and I knew his wife, Anne, well, but nothing would convince Checho that I had not publicly cuckolded my husband. Peter was highly amused by the whole episode, and even tried to explain it to the indignant Checho, but I never felt that I regained Checho's complete respect again.

More water

Now that we were back in Chile again, the weather was colder and often wetter. Frequently, we were driving through swirling mists. We had to pull out the bag containing our warmer clothes. Although before I opened it I wiped off the deep layer of Patagonian dust and grit, it soon became clear that the bag had acted as a container for our clothing but had not protected it. As well as itches and irritations caused by the various insects which had made our clothing a home, the clothes had also acquired skin-exfoliating properties due to being impregnated with sandy grit.

Once over the Andes, the stark contrast between the windy and dusty Argentina in the west and the wet, lush green Chile in the east was one of the surprises of southern Patagonia. Suddenly, geography lessons about how rain-laden clouds dump their payload when unable to rise over tall mountains all made sense.

At the base of every mountain was a raging torrent of water, so it was important that the two vehicles had excellent braking capacity. It was therefore a great shock when, going steeply downhill on an unmade road, Checho announced to Peter and me, sitting next to him in the cab, that the brakes on the van weren't working. As the dense forest flashed past on either side, and Checho used the gears to slow us down, there seemed to be little to do but pray for a side road to appear going back up the mountain. Fortunately, the brakes somehow re-engaged before we reached the river.

The terrain and the extreme weather conditions make building and maintaining bridges for a tiny population uneconomic, and so there were few bridges across the rivers then in southern Chile. Instead, there were small ferries capable of carrying a single car, or two horses. Each ferry was threaded onto a strong cable attached to both banks, and the reaction of the current of the river against the tethering is what propels the vessel. The roads here were almost all unmade and filled with potholes, so the intermittent braking ability of the campervan continued to be a worry. It reached fever pitch each time Checho drove onto a ferry, which had no guard rails. If he could not stop the campervan, it would roll across the small ferry, which had no protective barriers, and plunge straight into the icy torrent.

Many discussions were held to decide on the best course of action. There was nowhere nearby to get the brakes fixed, and to reach a town large enough to have a mechanic meant either travelling back to Coyhaique, where no brake cable might be available, or forward to our equidistant destination, Chaiten. A third option was just to stay by the side of the road, while some of the party drove into a town to hire a mechanic and bring him out to the campervan. This was quickly vetoed as we had no idea whether any mechanic would agree to such a plan. We decided to proceed cautiously. Our efforts to be safe severely hampered our progress.

At the top of any steep descent, everyone would decant into the typically drenching rain. Often Pedro, looking out for me, would use a machete to cut me a leaf from the giant rhubarb (*gunnera tinctoria*) plant. Each leaf was the size of a golf umbrella. Even though they were quite heavy to hold for long periods of time, they kept the rain from pouring down your face, and blurring your vision, getting in your mouth when you spoke, and running down your neck.

The walkers would walk down the hill trying to identify any gaps in the forest or trail entrances that Checho could turn into if the campervan brakes failed during descent. Someone would have to run back up the hill to tell Checho of the emergency plan, and eventually we would see poor Checho drive past us alone in the campervan, mouth set in a grim line of concentration, willing the brakes to engage.

From Coyhaique to Chaiten was an amazingly scenic journey but it was disappointing from the trapping perspective. The mountain sides were steep, and great long scars showed where the forests had been felled. In some parts, the mountainside looked like a giant plucked turkey. The natural habitat of the *monitos* was likely to have been disturbed. It was hard to know where to lay the traps, especially given the steep and slippery forest floor. None of the locals we passed had seen *monitos* in the bamboo or in the forests, and despite extensive searching, we only found evidence of one old *monito* nest in the bamboo.

At just a week into the trip, David and Tony were still very optimistic of success in trapping. But after four nights of laying 160 traps in rain and low cloud cover produced only about six mice per night, even their spirits were low, and some personal tensions became evident.

David had commented on his arrival that, although I looked more tanned than he had ever seen me, he had never seen me look so exhausted. At the time, I put it down to the fact that I always felt worried about basic survival. Would we have enough water until we could find a river? Would the water be safe to drink? Could we get the sleeping bags and tent dry by tonight? If it was ten days since we had any fruit or veg, were we in danger of scurvy? However, after those four days of trapping, David said he now understood why I looked exhausted all the time.

In addition to the hard physical work, the diet, he said, was appalling. David and Tony both complained about it, even though Peter and I thought it had improved dramatically since they had joined the group! The fact that Tony had made a significant financial contribution to the trip was also a factor, but our remoteness also meant that it was not often possible to find food to purchase. In David and Tony's food frustrations, I could recognise myself two months ago. The limited volume of food, the constant starch, the lack of fresh fruit and vegetables were insufficient for the heavy physical work we did. I had come to accept it, but recognised that I now had a different relationship to food. I saw food as a fuel and little more. It was a big contrast to before the trip, when I had been something of a foodie. I loved to cook and to eat. In fact, Peter and I belonged to a gourmet club, where the same group of eight friends took turns to cook each other extravagant meals every couple of months.

The field trip had opened my eyes not only to the limited availability of food which was reality for many people, but to the extent of my privileged life. For the first few weeks of the trip, I saw myself as walking in the footsteps of other pioneer-type women, who suffered hardships with forbearance as a matter of survival, and I relished the chance to try to meet that standard.

By halfway through the trip, I had definitely become more resilient and resourceful. But by the end of the trip, I felt almost ashamed at the ease of our life in Australia and all that we took for granted. The feeling was long-lasting.

Many months after our return home, my parents were visiting us for a meal. As I served the very basic food on odd cracked or chipped plates and handed everyone a fork, my mother asked me why I had not unpacked our kitchenware that had been in storage during our trip. I said that I didn't think we needed it, we had the basics and that was enough. She quietly pointed out that some people might perceive my new attitude as eccentric. Even though I had had a life-changing experience, she said, unless I was planning to move to Patagonia, it might be time to face the reality of my life in my world again, and conform just a little.

Although the arrival of two extra men had meant that I was not required to do as much heavy work in laying, checking and collecting traps through the dense wet forest, the additional people also meant there was more work in relation to collecting fresh water, and cooking, and support tasks. Tony and David also had their own studies for which they were collecting, weighing and measuring different animals, and Lucho was collecting insects which he needed to kill, preserve and mount. He still had a backlog of insects from Argentina which he needed to identify, so there was always masses of mess. In the evenings, Pedro would help with household duties while Checho and Lucho dealt with Lucho's insect collection. We all pitched in to make twice as much bait for the traps, as the wet conditions meant the bait dissolved in a few hours, and re-baiting each trap over a twenty-four hour period became important. We had to catch live moths and crickets for the *monitos* to eat, which was not always an easy task, as well as monitor their behaviour, weigh and measure them regularly, and clean their cage. We knew they were doing well, as the females began to build new nests. Whenever there was a free moment, we would dissect out the literally thousands of owl pellets, sorted into labelled bags to show the map coordinates of their origin. If any pellet produced the bones of a Patagonian opossum, we would know from where it came, and that could help to show the distribution of this little animal across Argentina (Birney et al. 1996).

Glacier

After the frustration of four days of poor trapping, we found a reasonable campsite beneath Ventisquero Colgante, a hanging glacier. I always imagined one would need to be very high up to even see a glacier, but here we were only about two hundred metres above sea level. Below the glacier, the river tumbled and shot over sharp-edged boulders. The glacier banks for quite some distance were pale rocks of all shapes and sizes. Distant mountains on both sides of our valley made it easy to visualise the downstream journey of the glacier as a river in ancient times. It also made one feel incredibly small, like an ant.

When the driving rain diminished to a drizzle, the whole group of us clambered upstream over the wet grey rocks to view the glacier up close. It was extraordinary, like a solid white giant frozen in time.

We had witnessed the awakening of another such giant a fortnight before as we drove by a silent lake with a glacier on the far side. A sudden sharp report in the stillness had made me search the blue sky for signs of lightning, only to hear and then see a mammoth chunk of glacier splash like the breaching of an enormous whale into the lake, creating a small tsunami.

Although this glacier was above a river and not a lake, in my usual anxious way I could still imagine being swept away if some of the glacier broke off, so it wasn't long before I headed back to camp alone. On my walk back, the rain began again, getting heavier and heavier. Now my imagination really began to get the better of me, and I wondered what to do if everyone else slipped off the rocks and were washed away by the river. I told myself that it was only my overactive imagination that sensed the river was getting higher. To prove to myself that I had nothing to worry about, I inserted a measuring stick into the edge of the river. As dusk began to close in, it soon became evident that the river was rising by about two inches per hour. I paced around, searching for any signs of movement of the others returning and was relieved to finally see them all. When I showed them my measuring stick, and suggested that we move camp to higher ground, they told me not to let my imagination get the better of me. Then they had what I privately called a men's meeting and decided to move our camp a little further away from the river. Checho and Peter continued to monitor the river every hour, and even though the rain began to lighten up at about ten p.m., it was agreed that someone would stay awake all night to keep watch in case the river rose more quickly.

Peter and I took the first watch from eleven p.m. to three a.m. The rain diminished to a slight drizzle and Peter managed to light a fire among the rocks a few metres from the river. Eventually, one by one, stars appeared in the sky, until breathtakingly, the sky became ablaze with stars of every shape and size. It was the first time I realised the extent and variation of the galaxies above. An enormous moon rose and bathed the river with light. Peter and I could have been the only people in the world.

It was very special to have some time alone to talk, as it was something which had rarely happened on the trip. Always the work needed to come first, and I knew that there was no time or space for me to be demanding of Peter's time. So on that bright moonlit night, sitting by the fire, I felt able to talk to him about some of my misgivings and frustrations, including having to wash in an icy river.

I complained of our dirty clothes and my dirty hair. One of the things we laughed about was that Checho had observed to me that my hair was magical, as it was brown at the roots but then seemed to become blonde further down. Peter asked me whether I had brought some hair dye with me (I had). In a scene reminiscent of the movie *Out of Africa*, and even though he had never done such a thing before, Peter applied bleach to the dark roots of my hair. After heating up several pans of hot water, he washed and rinsed and dried my hair by the fire.

This very romantic gesture culminated in me going to bed in the tent feeling clean, warm and loving, when Checho came on duty at three a.m. Peter said he would come to bed soon, but an hour later he was still sitting by the fire and talking while I waited and willed him to come to bed. Eventually, the pleasure and intimacy reflected in my clean and now blonder hair was replaced by intense sadness as I went to sleep alone. That was the first time we had had any time to ourselves for months. I really wanted his attention; I wanted him, and I knew it might be a long time before we shared any more time together alone.

In the morning, Checho reported that he and Peter had watched the river drop by a metre, and seen a Chilean pudu, a richly red-brown animal a bit like a pygmy deer, come really close to the river to drink as the sun rose. And even though I would have liked to witness both of those events, I felt jealous that Peter preferred to share the time with Checho rather than coming to bed with me. I really missed my husband, even though I was with him almost all of every day.

As the sun became warmer, we turned out all our wet clothes and sleeping bags and draped them over the rocks to dry. The men went out to check the traps they had laid the night before in the rain, but returned only with several leeches apiece. We spent the next several hours carefully inspecting their bodies and removing the bloodsuckers. It was interesting to see each individual's reaction to the leeches on their body – some were revolted and wanted to get rid of them as quickly as possible; so fast, in fact, that they singed their body hair when waving a flame over the leech. Peter, by contrast, laconically examined each leech and noted which ones had sucked more of his blood than their mates. I reflected sadly that Peter was always the scientist…even when a warm wife was on offer.

Chaiten to Chiloé

The arrival at Chaiten offered our first view of the sea since leaving La Madrugada in Argentina.

For once, we stayed in a proper camping ground, where Lucho and his team had stayed before, and it did much to restore the spirits of the group. Lucho chose a site he liked on the very edge of the ground, where we could make a large fire, and where we could be far away from the other campers. It was a clear starry night, we had lots of pisco sours, and we roasted a side of lamb for dinner. To our great delight, the campground manager joined us with four of his nine sons, and they serenaded us for a couple of hours with songs from South America.

Curiously, though, if there had been a photo of the event, it would have revealed some interesting things about the group. Three people were sitting in a row astride a log slightly back from the main group: me, with Pedro close in front of me, and Checho close behind me. I remember observing that neither of them felt very comfortable in this spontaneous campfire party. The arrival of the five very pleasant and outgoing Spanish locals dominated the attention of Lucho and the three Australian men. We three, two Indian men and a woman, were somehow marginalised and unable to participate in this interaction in some subtle, unspoken way. I am sure it would not have crossed Peter's or Tony's or David's minds that I might feel vulnerable or excluded, but as the only woman among eleven men, I felt grateful for Pedro's and Checho's body warmth, both literally and metaphorically. I had not previously observed Checho's and Pedro's Indian ethnicity making them feel marginalised. But I wondered whether they were sticking close to me to provide protection or to seek it.

Of course, like many camping grounds, this one had separate male and female toilet blocks. Given that the men in the group were not too fussed about where they urinated, the fact that our campsite was miles away from the toilet block bothered them not one iota. When I had asked before the arrival of our guests whether we had enough batteries for the torch to light my way to the female amenities block, I was horrified to hear Lucho say that they never ever bothered to use the toilet blocks, and if they were inside the campervan, they also didn't bother to go outside. They all simply took it in turns to pee in the sink. I tried not to think back on whether I had ever seen any of them clean the sink (I hadn't). I tried not to think of all the food I had prepared in the sink, and whether I had popped anything in my mouth that might have made contact with the sink while being rinsed (I had). Yuk.

Later that night when the wind came up strongly, I awoke in the campervan, busting to go to the toilet. I opened the door to walk the long distance to the amenities block but had second thoughts. All the men were asleep around the campfire, and the flames were casting creepy jumping shadows between the trees. I wondered if *el trauco* was a spirit or a human who hid in the forest. I closed the door again. I weed in the bucket, and carefully emptied it down the plughole in the sink.

The next morning, we all boarded a huge ferry for the nine-hour trip from Chaiten to Puerto Montt. Originally, we had thought we would be taking the ferry from Chaiten directly to Chiloé Island, but it transpired that that ferry only operated during high summer, so we now faced two ferry trips instead of just one to get to our new destination.

Despite it looking bigger than I had anticipated, I was not looking forward to the ferry trip, given my propensity for seasickness. As we waited to board, there was clear sunshine and a cold wind rippling the surface of the water in, for me, a rather stomach-churning way. Once the vehicles were loaded, most of the group went inside to sit and read. Checho, who also said he was prone to seasickness, and Peter and I went upstairs and sat outside in the lifeboat, in the sun and wind.

This was to be the most beautiful journey. The Chilean coastline was magnificent, with huge forests right down to the water. For the first half of the trip, the sea, unbelievably, was like a mirror. I could never have imagined a sea so still. (Always the panic merchant, I even fleetingly wondered if we were somehow in the eye of an enormous storm.) It was surreal to be moving slowly through what appeared to be glass and leaving barely a ripple behind us. I enjoyed spicy sausage and local baked beans (which was what the crew also had for lunch), before returning to doze in the lifeboat in the sun through the second half of the journey, during which there was only a slight swell. We disembarked in Puerto Montt, quickly bought some supplies, and boarded the second ferry, which took only thirty minutes to make its way to Chiloé Island, where we arrived on Tuesday, 15 December 1985.

Chiloé felt like a magical place. Around a hundred and ninety kilometres from north to south, not only is it a beautiful island, seemingly untouched by so-called Western development, but it was reknowned for its fresh seafood. We sampled it in a restaurant in El Fogon. That meal, with its fresh crab, perfectly cooked fish and crunchy salad (heaven!) remains one of the most memorable meals of my life.

On our first full day there, we were happy to sit in a café by the sea at Castro, one of the three towns on the island, while waiting for the *camionetta* repairs. I had an empanada for breakfast, Peter had fresh crab, and Checho had steak and juice. The waiter, when he brought the coffee, proudly told us the milk was directly from a cow on Chiloé, which probably meant it was unpasteurised. The cows, along with the rich chocolate soil, drizzling rain, and an abundance of apple trees, reminded us of Tasmania. And in common with people everywhere who live on islands, it seems, the locals could not have been more friendly.

The next day, we split into two groups, with Lucho, Tony, David and Pedro taking the campervan and laying traps at Lake Tepelhueco, while Checho, Peter and I took the *camionetta* on a long drive across the island, making enquiries of the locals about whether they had ever seen *monitos*. It was fascinating, firstly because we had to speak in Spanish the whole time, and secondly because of the vast array of different personalities we encountered. We drove along the roads, stopping and asking people in the fields or in little houses if they knew of or had seen *monitos*. As we talked to the locals in Chiloé, we found many of them were fearful or suspicious about discussing *monitos*.

We could not use the Spanish name of *monito del monte*, as the locals called the animals by the Indian name of *chumaihuen*. A woodcutter in Molulco said that he had not seen any for fifteen years, but he had once found one in a hole in a tree trunk. At Chadmo Central, a man said he found one years ago and he kept it but it died. He had not given it food, as he believed it was the spirit of the forest. He told us the Mapuche name for the animal was *amayhual*.

At Yaldad, an old man on a horse and leading a second horse told us these animals lived inside the trunks of trees, and that there was a second kind of related animal, which was bigger and fought with dogs. Also in Yaldad, a young boy named Silvio had found an animal in a tree trunk in the forest, and kept it for two weeks, after which it died. They had not thought it necessary to give it food, as they believed it was a spirit. After its death, Silvio and his friend Ramon dried the skin, which we bought for a thousand pesos, or about five Australian dollars.

A man with a child near Colonia Yungay said he had heard of a ball falling out of a tree and becoming such an animal. A man, standing by the bridge at Chaighou when we spoke to him, said he had found an animal twenty years ago near Colonia Yungay and taken it home. He fed it sugared water for two weeks, and when it became debilitated he took it to the local hospital, but he did not know what became of it.

Two years ago, a man in Huillinco had found a *chumaihuen* nest in a tree with one animal. He took it home, but did not feed it, and it died. He described the animal as *muy bravo*, very brave, suggesting it had put up some kind of fight. Other responses included that these animals were rare or hidden, and were only known to live in piles of *palos* or logs. Generally, responses to questions were very guarded, but it was not until we spoke to a local Indigenous headman in Correo Quellon that we understood why. He said the animal was considered mysterious, as it disappears, and it was the subject of many strong myths. It was rumoured to bring good luck and gold to those who had one, but only if its captive status was kept secret from everyone but the owner. He subsequently had one of his workers ask a very old aunt what she knew of these animals, and when she heard the word *chumaihuen*, her face 'closed over, she placed her hand over her mouth, and she became suspicious'. (Field notes from 15 December 1985)

So it became clear, as we travelled around Chiloe, that the animals' spiritual status was unquestioned, as those who had tried to keep them in captivity for good luck believed they did not require food. It was hard not to feel saddened by the likely cause of death for these little animals whose captors innocently believed they were taking good care of them.

A woodcutter at Piriquina was one of the few people we spoke to who did not seem hesitant to discuss the animals. In his twenty-two years as a woodcutter, he had seen many animals in the *chusqea* behind his house. In cutting down the forest, and burning the wood, he not infrequently found animals hiding in the bamboo. He also referred to the animals as *perrito del monte* (little dog of the forest) because of the shape of the face and the cold nose.

A visit to the national park office at Cucau was valuable, as the ranger there had found five *monitos* two weeks earlier in a single nest. They were all almost adults, and the ranger had photographed them before releasing them back into the park. Compared to our travelling *monitos*, the five had enormously fat tails, and very hairy ears which were folded forward. They also appeared to be much whiter on the belly. It was impossible to know whether they were a subspecies of the mainland *monitos* or not.

The visit to the park ranger left us feeling a little optimistic for our future trapping success. It was just somewhat disturbing then to find that we had run out of peanut butter, that we used in the bait recipe, and that nowhere on the island could we find any. After much discussion and testing of alternatives for odour, consistency and resistance to dissolving effects of steady rain, Peter came up with a new bait recipe which included mashed tinned sardines.

Given that we were rolling bait every day, and sometimes twice a day, the sardine oil had a definite benefit on the skin of my hands, which were weather-beaten and constantly covered in scratches. It was also, however, impossible to get rid of the odour, as we had little water for hand washing. When mixed with the smell of the gore of dissections, and the urine in the animal cages while being cleaned out, the sardine oil was just too overpowering, and I often had to quell an urge to gag. I was amazed that after a few days I didn't even notice and could carry on as normal; testimony to the adaptive powers of the human body!

In one end and out the other

There are two very clear memories I have of Chiloé. When Peter and Checho and I were travelling alone, one night we stopped at a village next to a stony beach within walking distance of a tiny slab-built hotel. As we set up camp, Peter made the comment that, with absolutely no houses to be seen, it seemed a bit like a one-horse town. When we later approached the hotel, to our great amusement, there was one saddled horse tied up to the railing outside the hotel!

Peter and I ate a simple meal of fish and potatoes at the little hotel, which had a swept dirt floor, a few tables and chairs, and a tiny battery-operated TV in one corner. To our surprise when we walked in, playing on the TV was an episode of a miniseries based in India which Peter and I had watched just before leaving Australia. In the story, the widow of an Indian man was required to perform suttee; be burned alive on his funeral pyre.

As she walked to her death, the mourners observing her chanted, 'Brum, brum. Brum, brum.' It seemed extraordinary to be watching a TV show, dubbed in Spanish, about Indian culture, in a remote area of southern Chile. It reminded me of the time a decade before, when I was travelling with my own parents and siblings in what was then Rhodesia, in Africa. We stayed in a small rural hotel and when we walked into the communal lounge, the Australian TV series *Skippy the Bush Kangaroo* was playing on the TV. I guess people everywhere are fascinated by people of other cultures.

Soon after the widow was burned on the fire, the episode finished, and a sports program began, featuring boxing. Out of nowhere, it seemed, suddenly the bar was full of many local men glued to the tiny TV screen. When Peter and I emerged into the night, there was an entire row of horses tied up to the railing! In the absence of any lights to be seen in the darkness, it was hard to know from where all the men had come. Being on horseback was probably a great advantage, though, for when the drinkers rolled out of the bar some hours later, they climbed onto horses which probably required no direction to get them home safely.

Checho had disappeared as soon as we set up camp, and we did not see him again until morning. He offered no explanation of where he had been, and nor did he need to. At the time, my view was that he was offering me some time alone with Peter, for which I was very grateful, but with the cynicism of mature age, I now suspect he wanted a break from us and sought out some other company.

The other event I remember clearly on Chiloé Island was not so pleasant, as it was my fault and it upset Lucho rather badly.

The whole crew was camped again together at Lake Tepelhueco and Lucho was very excited as there was a particular insect he was hoping to trap. He had been talking about the insect throughout the trip and he was clearly very hopeful of success when we arrived, as both the season and the weather seemed to be providing ideal conditions for catching his prey.

And indeed the weather was beautiful. We had a couple of sunny days in a row, and on the second day I decided to go down to the lake's edge and give myself a good clean-up, and then do some much-needed washing. Checho and Peter went to lay traps far away from the lake, and as I left the campsite at lunchtime, Lucho told me that he, Pedro, David and Tony would soon take the campervan for a drive into the town and would be back for dinner.

By the lake, there was no one about. Even though the water was cold, the sun was hot and there was no breeze, so I washed my hair, myself and our clothes. For once, I felt very content. I walked slowly back to the campsite. I spread the washing on the surrounding low bushes to dry. And it was then that I made a horrible discovery. Barely hidden beneath a beautiful flowering bush was a very tidy but enormous and foul-smelling pile of human poo. How disgusting! Not even thirty metres from our campsite! I could scarcely believe it. Among our group, the rules were that you took the little spade with the roll of toilet paper threaded on the handle, and you went at least two hundred metres away from camp to dig a decent hole, defecate and bury it. Had this been left by a local who was trying to warn us off?

No one else was home and I could not leave that irksome pile just sitting there. I fetched the spade and dug a good hole beside it, and then with sticks I managed to transfer it into the hole. I covered it with soil, and just for good measure I covered the site with mulch from the surrounding forest. I found it hard to get the smell out of my nostrils, so I even washed the spade.

Then, tired from all my exertions, I lay down in the back of the *camionetta* with the rear door open, and fell asleep in the hot sun. Some time later, I became vaguely aware of Peter's voice and then I heard Checho say, in Spanish, *'Ella esta aqui, dormiendo como una princessa.* (She is here sleeping, like a princess.)' I allowed myself to drift off to sleep again.

When I woke, it was dusk and Peter was sitting beside me in the *camionetta*. To my surprise, he was asking if I had seen a pile of poo near the campsite. How did he know about that? Had someone been watching me and then told him?

He gently broke the news to me that it was Lucho's poo. (I experienced a flash of admiration for his gut; clearly not affected by the almost total lack of fibre in our diet!) Apparently, the special insect was only attracted by a combination of colour and odour, and Lucho had spent several days modifying his own diet to achieve and locate alongside a particular species of flowering tree what would have surely been an orgasmic feast for the hapless insect. Oh, the humiliation!

Peter was torn between amusement at the situation, and regret for Lucho, a fellow scientist whose extreme efforts had been ruined by an ignorant and busybody female, who should not have been on a men's field trip in the first place! It took all of my courage to attempt to apologise to Lucho, who waved me away with a cold look. For the rest of the night, Pedro and Checho behaved as if there had been a death in the family, and David and Tony did not make eye contact with me. It crossed my mind that they probably all had discussed the project and anticipated successfully trapping the insect in a men's conversation from which I was excluded. It was a hard lesson. When it came to the trapping, I was expected, and indeed happy, to contribute. But I was not a natural scientist like the others, and I was not one of the boys, and I should not have meddled in things I didn't understand.

Fortunately, the next day, David and Tony broke the tension when they found a shrew opossum in their trapline. It was very exciting, even though it proved to be a female and could not provide a sperm sample. A colleague from a Chilean TV station had asked us to bring any uncommon marsupials we caught back to civilisation with us, as he was shooting a wildlife series. So Maxine, as we called her in memory of Max, became a travelling shrew opossum, and ultimately was the star of her own short film a couple of weeks later. She was a remarkable animal who had seventeen teats, the most that Peter had ever seen on a marsupial. And given that the previous world record for keeping a shrew opossum in captivity was only a matter of hours for poor Max, we were subsequently very proud that we were able to maintain Maxine's health.

Lago Chapo revisited

Just before Christmas, we returned to Lago Chapo for a week, and camped near the family with whom I had spent my birthday in October. We had access to the river that ran by their house for drinking and cooking. I noticed many more signs of cowpats in and around the river than on our previous trip, but by now I was becoming immune to my fears about dirty water. At least in Chile all the streams were fast-flowing, although Lucho pointed out that one could never tell what was being put into the water upstream, out of sight.

The decision had been made to lay traps on the mountain we had visited on my birthday, in the hopes of catching some more *monitos*, a decision which committed us to a lot of driving, rowing and climbing to both lay and check the traps. On the first day, I went to help carry and lay out the traps. I rowed across and back and was flattered when Tony, who had been a cox in his younger years, said I had good wrist action! In retrospect, I imagine he may have struggled to find something positive to say about my rowing, but I was so happy with the compliment! Even though he could have made the same comment to one of the men, it somehow made me feel more female, and appreciated.

Checking the traps under such conditions was tough. It was bad enough to have to walk long distances twice a day under any conditions, but rowing and climbing up the mountain side made it really hard work and very time-consuming. Apart from millions of mice, the only *monito* success, if you can call it that, was a female *monito* found in a snap trap with four tiny bald babies in her pouch. She, sadly, was dead. The babies were alive but had absolutely no chance of survival without any fur, or milk, or mother, and so the sad decision was made to help send them into the long sleep. Later, they gained scientific fame as part of a study on pouch development in *monitos*.

Fortunately, the weather was fine, although uncharacteristically windy. But it wasn't long before I was missing the cold and damp, as with the sun came what seemed to be a plague of the aggressive horseflies which stung painfully. When Lucho told me not get upset by them but to take my anger out by catching and eating them, I thought he must be mad. But then he showed me how to catch one. He broke off its head, and extracted a little bag of honey which was around the ovaries of the fly. It was really delicious, and the absence of sugar in our diet led to my decision to decapitate any flies that managed to bite me. Interestingly, I got tired of this game far more rapidly than the March flies, which landed in droves on any exposed skin. We all carried the marks of the stings for weeks afterwards.

I was interested to see that a little more progress had been made on the house of our friends; they now had an enormous photo of the Pope adorning the main room! There also seemed to be a few extra chairs. A couple of nights before Christmas, the family invited us to share a traditional feast called a *curanto*.

A large hole was dug outside the house, and it was lined with hot stones which had been heating in a roaring fire nearby. On top of the hot stones were placed every type of shellfish, including giant deepwater barnacles known as *picorojos* (literally 'red penises'), whole fish, chicken, potatoes, onions and bread. The whole lot was covered then with leaves and turf. During the several hours this feast took to cook, a large quantity of wine was consumed by the men, who hung around outside by the fire and interacted the way people of all cultures do at a barbecue.

However, the women remained inside, or well out of the men's way, and even though I was a woman, I was a visitor, and so I was automatically treated like one of the men. When the men sat down, they insisted I join them, even though I would have preferred the company of the women. The men all treated me with courtesy but did not speak to me directly, so I was surprised when we all stood up to take a group photo, that one of the young men standing next to me boldly groped me! I was even more surprised when I moved away from him and stood near someone else, and the same thing happened again. Later, when I asked Checho about it, he said that the Indian men were under the impression, from TV, that Western women were hungry for such activity! I felt lucky to have ended the evening with nothing more intrusive than a grope…

On Christmas Eve, we drove into Puerto Montt to put Checho on the bus to Santiago, so he could spend Christmas with his family. We had a lovely lunch in a restaurant before driving back to the campsite. On the way, we passed some eucalyptus trees, and we stopped and broke off a branch to serve as our Christmas tree. Once back at the campsite, as I had been unable to buy wrapping paper in town, I wrapped some little gifts for the others in paper towels.

We were having a drink by the fire at about ten p.m., when one of the Indian boys came to say he had found a sheep to buy for Christmas dinner, and could we pay for it and drive to collect it? So Lucho and Pedro drove off in the *camionetta* to collect it. They didn't return until almost midnight, having dropped the (live) sheep off to the family for despatching in the morning. So we then had a small toast of whisky, and a slice of *pan de Pascua* (an Easter loaf of dried fruit and nuts), which is traditional fare, apparently, at Christmas. Lucho told us that Easter is not always celebrated as a separate event in Chile, and so Easter eggs are available in the shops at Christmas time.

We exchanged small gifts. I received a cassette of Andean music from Checho, a little straw *trauco* doll I had wanted from Peter, some marzipan from Lucho, and a toy stuffed dog from Pedro. We finally got to bed very late, but we still needed to be up very early to row across the lakes, climb the mountain and check the traps before joining our friends for lunch at eleven a.m.

As well as the six of us, there were three families at the house for lunch. As each family had eight to ten members, it amounted to quite an event.

They kindly fed we gringos first at the table. We started with barbecued lamb, which had been marinated in wine, fresh coriander and oil. There was salad of tomato and onion with fresh coriander, lettuce and snap peas with dressing, fresh homemade bread and boiled potatoes. Dessert was tinned peaches, with wild raspberries. After we had eaten our lunch, we left the table, and a second sitting of men began theirs. I didn't see the women sit to eat, they were on standby in the kitchen at all times, and if they ate, they did it standing up, as all the chairs were outside.

Afternoon tea was served at around six thirty p.m., with coffee and cakes – one large cake provided by each family. At afternoon tea time, unlike at lunchtime, all of the men from all the families sat down together, so there I was again with fifteen men. This time, however, as soon as I had finished my cake and coffee, the señora asked if I would like to go in by the stove where it was warmer, even though the evening was very warm. From that, I assumed that now my status as visitor had been honoured, it was time to accept my place in the kitchen with the other women. A very welcome relief for me!

In the evening after the other two families had left, the señora asked Peter and me if we would accept her seven-year-old son as a gift. At first, I thought I had misunderstood her Spanish, and when I questioned if I had heard correctly, Lucho said she was asking if we would agree to be *padrinos* (godparents). I explained that we were not Catholic, but she said that was not important. Furthermore, she said she had asked Peter two years ago when he was in Lago Chapo, although he had no recollection of it.

We asked what was involved, but apparently we would not even be required to be present at the baptismal ceremony. Later that night, Lucho explained that being a *padrino* was a euphemism for investing financially in a child and paying for their education. We both would have been happy to be a sponsor of some kind, but we explained to Lucho that we did not know what commitment we could make when we still had not started a family of our own. He offered to explain it to her, and it was not mentioned again.

Christmas Day ended with music. The battery-powered radio was turned on and to the Chilean folk music, people began to dance a polka-like folk dance. It was great fun. After we had a cup of hot chocolate made with milk straight from the cow (a Christmas tradition there), we said our farewells. Some of the young men in the family went out to a party and returned at about one a.m. to our campsite, well after we had all gone to bed. In the morning when we woke up, there were extra bodies squeezed in everywhere, in the tents, the camper and the *camionetta*! It was very strange but somehow festive, and a good end to our first Chilean Christmas. It was only much later that I wondered whether Checho had told them about my sleeping with David in his tent. Perhaps they had thought that if they came to the campsite they might end up with a Christmas present from me!

Puyehue 2

Just after Christmas we headed back to Puyehue National Park to stay in the A-frame hut I had criticised the first time for its substandard amenities. Now a couple of months later, it felt like a five-star hotel. It was also so much jollier than last time as we all knew each other better, and we were able to easily get regular supplies of food.

We also had Tony and David to assist with the trapping, so the work that had been done on our last visit by Checho, Peter and me now had two more sets of hands. I also quite liked the fact that Tony and David, new to the area, still found making their way through the forest, and laying and checking traps to be challenging. I was an old hand, who could offer advice about directions and the location of the river, and what to do when attacked by the nasty biting horseflies.

The horseflies were abundant, and nimble, so both skin-covering clothing (preferably not blue, which seemed to be especially attractive), and brandishing a leaf swat was essential. The sun was out until about nine thirty p.m., but fortunately the horseflies went to bed at around four p.m. as the temperature dropped, so there was a period of a few hours a day when being outside was seriously pleasant.

At last I really felt like I had time to look around and enjoy my surroundings. Lucho had told us that we should be able to see torrent ducks in the river. Torrent ducks are unusual because they hold territory in fast flowing rivers usually above 1,500 metres. They can swim up against the rapids, but rarely fly. Unlike many birds, the female is more colourful than the male.

One day, Peter, Checho and I ventured close to the rapids at the Salta de Princessa (Princess Falls). Now the weather was not so freezing we could spend a little time standing still and waiting. Our patience was rewarded. A pair of torrent ducks suddenly appeared. They almost appeared to be running on the surface of the water as they headed upstream over the rapids – a truly amazing sight. I felt so privileged to be able to witness it, and to contribute to the telling of the event to David and Tony. Their interest in my observations made me perceive a small shift in my position on the team. I now saw glimmers of myself as a scientific contributor, however novice, and no longer a burden.

This awareness was augmented the next day when, in his typically mysterious way, Checho brought into the camp with him with a strange young Indian man, who spoke neither English nor Spanish. He had told Checho in the local dialect that he knew exactly where to locate some *monitos*' nests in the forest, up above the Pampa del Sol on the side of Volcan Cabulco.

Peter was very busy fixing specimens. It is a task that cannot wait as once an animal has died, any specimens which are to be preserved need to be fixed straight away. Peter asked Checho and me to go with the young man to check out the nests. I remember feeling proud that Peter thought I would be an acceptable substitute for him as far as recording the details of the search were concerned, and I was determined not let him down.

After a drive of thirty minutes or so, we parked the *camionetta* at the end of a road, and walked for an hour or more through low rainforest until we came to a high plain. It was then that I realised how far away from camp we were – in fact, how far away we were from any signs of human habitation at all – and I became slightly uneasy. The Pampa del Sol, an open meadow, was incredibly beautiful. Tall green grass was sprinkled with colourful wildflowers gently swaying in the breeze. In the crystal-clear air and bright sunlight of the Andes, the colours were so vibrant that they almost seemed to sparkle.

Just higher than the pampa was the forest proper, which similarly seemed like a magical place – tall evergreens and massive Magellanic fuchsia bushes over twenty feet high. It was eerily quiet, and although Checho and I could be heard cracking twigs underfoot as we followed the young man into the forest, he made not a single sound. When I realised that, I must admit to some anxiety as it crossed my mind that the young man could easily lose us. I tried to keep myself from imagining us meeting horrible deaths at the hand of this mysterious youth or his compatriots who maybe were secreted away in this silent forest.

After thirty minutes of walking, during which I did not let him out of my sight, Checho suddenly stopped and pointed to the young man, who stood motionless beneath what was clearly a nest. Made of *Chusquea culeou*, the beautiful type of bamboo found only in South America, the nest was high off the ground in the fork of the native Chilean pitra tree (*myrceugenia exsucca*), in a spot that would get the little sun that filtered through. A carefully constructed ball of tightly overlapping leaves which would prevent permeation of rain into the nest, it looked like a cosy little home. The entrance hole was small and pointed downwards. It seemed incredible to think that these tiny marsupials could build it.

This particular nest was lined with moss and fern, but was empty and looked as if it was not currently used. Over the next couple of hours, we found several more nests but there were no residents at home. I carefully took detailed notes describing the nests and their positions. As the long shadows of the late afternoon began appearing, the young man made it clear he needed to go, and he slipped away as silently as he had appeared. As he left, I once again felt anxious. There I was, alone with Checho in a remote and thick forest with no idea of the way out. I was with a man I trusted but who spoke no English, and my Spanish was very unsophisticated. What if I became separated from Checho? Or he fell and broke his leg? How would I find my way to safety?

I need not have worried. Checho led us out safely to the Pampa del Sol. Once we reached there, he suggested a brief rest, and he lay back in the grass and closed his eyes. It occurred to me that maybe he had been stressed too, with having the responsibility of me. I lay down in the grass near him. Perhaps because of the tension of the preceding few hours spent in the gloom of the forest, I was filled with a tremendous sense of well-being as we basked in warmth of the late afternoon sun, surrounded by long grass and wildflowers rippling in the gentle breeze.

Looking through the field notes now, I came across some pages which have been stuck in with sticky tape. In my pencilled handwriting, the notes describe the location of eight different nests we subsequently found near the traplines. I can see that I had observed that we often found two nests reasonably close together. In the notes, I wrote the question, is it possible that there are two nests together always? One for the males and one for the females and babies? I wonder whether anyone yet knows the answer.

Goodbye David

During the day of New Year's Eve, David returned to Australia. We took him into Osorno, a city from which he was able to catch a bus to Santiago to fly home. I was sad to see him go, not least because his presence had taken some of the burden off me to contribute to the trapping. He looked very happy to be going home to be reunited with his new wife.

After we waved the bus off, Peter and I took the rare opportunity to behave like regular tourists and wander around the market. Colourful to both eyes and ears, and filled with tempting aromas interwoven with less appealing smells of live fish and fresh meat, the market was all one could have hoped for. There were handknitted items like socks, jumpers and ponchos competing for hanging space with baskets and woven straw objects of all shapes and sizes. There was local and imported pottery, alongside stalls of fresh herbs, and interspersed with stalls selling cheap items of the kind found in tourist markets the world over. There were stalls selling unfamiliar cuts of meat and great cauldrons of fresh and cooked shellfish. There was beautiful handmade silver jewellery, as well as items made of leather. I bought some tiny black pottery items, doll's size versions of jugs and cups, decorated in white. I still have them.

We treated ourselves to corn *humitas*, fragrant and sweet freshground corn which has been flavoured and cooked in the corn leaves. When we came to pay for them, Peter realised that he had $400 less in his pocket than he thought he had. We never solved the mystery of that money, but we both left the market feeling out-of-sorts. It put a dampener on a day that had otherwise been fun. My pleasure at being part of the real world again was supplanted by an overwhelming urge to get back to the campsite and away from civilisation.

Lucho suggested that to celebrate New Year's Eve we should go to a dinner dance being held at the café attached to the national park information centre. He explained that the event was usually held only for staff, but because we had been staying for a while, they were happy for us to attend. I was very pleased at the thought of a meal prepared by others, and which would hopefully include some vegetables.

We walked over from our hut in the dark at eight p.m. We didn't have anything different from our everyday clothes to wear, so I tried to make myself feel a bit festive by putting my hair up into a ponytail. Although we had all had a good wash, we must still have looked a little out of place for a festive event.

The venue was very simply decorated and the tables were set for about thirty people. We sat there for several minutes on our own, and then suddenly the room was full of people. I had no idea that there were so many staff, as we had never previously seen them. I was relieved to see that the only sign of dressing up for some of the men was that their hair was combed back with hair gel. I was especially pleased to see there were a handful of women, of varying ages; short, sturdy women with shrill voices who were clearly ready for a good time.

I don't recall the meal, but the moment the dinner was over, the music was turned up full volume and talking was no longer possible. In a fashion typical of many cultures, the women got up to dance, and several men, including Lucho and Tony, decided it was time to retire. After much pleading from the women on the dance floor, Peter and Checho and I joined them. Peter's and my dancing caused much hilarity amongst the others. Most of the people on the dance floor were doing folk dancing, with lots of footwork, one hand on hip and the other held high in the air. Even though the music was unfamiliar, it had a strong and steady beat, and so Peter and I just danced as we would always dance at home. The other dancers clapped and laughed and as the evening wore on we all became good friends, even though we struggled to understand each other with the different dialects and loud music. As midnight approached, the dancing became more and more frenetic, and the women cried out, *'Que rico, que rico'* (how rich, meaning 'what fun') to demonstrate their glee. Then it was midnight, and the music was turned off, and everyone exchanged hugs and kisses, and disappeared silently into the darkness. Peter and I walked in the dark to our hut, talking about past New Year's Eves.

I went to bed wondering what we would be doing next New Year's Eve. Whenever we had met new people on this trip, inevitably I was asked where my children were, and people were surprised and sometimes even shocked to see a woman of my age with no children. It had made me speculate about how tough it would be to be a childless woman in Chile.

Truthfully on this trip, I had been hoping to get pregnant. I had had two miscarriages before we came away, and I had somewhat foolishly thought that this 'holiday' from our usual work might do the trick for a successful pregnancy. But I had not accounted for the communal sleeping situation. Very early on, it became clear that the suspension in the campervan reacted squeakily and loudly to anyone even rolling over in bed. The back of the *camionetta* was small, uncomfortable and hard, although not as unforgiving as a tent or forest floor. But even if we could have found a comfortable place, we were both constantly tired from the hard physical labour involved in almost all everyday activities such as collecting water, let alone the trapping. Nothing quells ardour like exhaustion.

And of course, it takes two to tango. Achieving time alone with Peter was easier said than done. We rarely went to bed at the same time, as he was often up late in the night processing animals. The moment his head hit the pillow he was asleep, and snoring. Loudly. This was one of the reasons I tried to go to bed and to sleep before he arrived, as otherwise I would lie awake for hours resenting the noise. It seemed that for now, at least, a baby was out of the question.

Puyehue 3

Early in the New Year, there was great excitement when we learnt that a group of film-makers were coming to Puyehue to film our *monitos* for a television documentary. Peter and I had met Sergio Nunez and some of his team from the natural history unit of Canal 7 in Chile when they came to Australia the preceding year to film some Australian animals.

Peter, Tony and Checho worked hard just outside our hut to set up a confined area of natural forest where the *monitos* could be released safely, without escaping, but still be seen by the cameras. I was happy to carry on with my cleaning and washing chores, but also eager to see how the film-makers would set up their equipment. So I had the door to the hut open so I could keep an eye on progress outside.

Just before the film-makers were due to arrive at twelve, I saw through the open door a local man on a horse, leading another horse behind him. Checho greeted him briefly and then took the reins of the second horse and walked it over to the hut. He called me, and told me that he had organised for me to have the horse for a couple of hours so that I could go riding. He indicated that I should hop on and get going.

This was one of those moments when I wondered what I had lost in translation at some earlier point in time. It was clear that Checho had organised it as a gift of some kind. But it was not a gift I really wanted! I had only ever been on a horse once in my life before, and not only was I slightly nervous of horses, but I was allergic to horsehair! I couldn't imagine why Checho would think that I would be keen for a ride, except that he himself loved horses, and so perhaps thought everyone did. Besides that, I was looking forward to seeing the filming.

The horse seemed docile enough. The leather of the bridle was beautifully carved but well-worn. There was no saddle, but a woollen blanket was tied on over a hessian sack. The stirrups were each made of a single carved piece of wood in the shape of a short clog. We had seen gauchos in Argentina using the same types of stirrups. Gauchos also wore shoes with terrifying jagged black metal spurs attached to the back, which could be seen protruding from the clog-stirrups.

Checho indicated I should get on the horse. I couldn't imagine how I was going to get up there. He led the horse over to a low fence and suggested that I mount the horse from there, successfully saving me from what I am sure would have been many ugly attempts to mount. But before I had time to even say a few words, Checho was distracted by the arrival of Sergio and his team, and he rushed to call the rest of our team, who all arrived at a run. No one seemed to be able to hear me call out to them, or perhaps they didn't want to. They was much backslapping, and hilarity, as greetings and introductions were made, and then they all went inside the hut to make a cup of coffee.

Through all of this, I was sitting high up on the horse, but I might as well have been on another planet. No one took any notice of me at all. That included the horse. Despite my best efforts of pleading and yelling by turns, I could not get the horse to do anything. It put its head down and munched the grass, and only moved when it judged another patch to be juicier.

I have no idea how long I was on the horse but it was way too long. By the time the men came out of the hut, the horse had moved some distance away, with me a captive on its back. I had thought of climbing down, but was worried that if I did the horse might bolt off and become lost. I could hear the men as they went off to do their filming. The warmth of the sun was fading when finally Checho came looking for me. I was probably only half a kilometre from the hut. It occurred to me that Peter probably had no idea of where I was, but as usual did not seem to be missing me enough to look for me. Checho just laughed when I said I had not been able to control the horse. He jumped up behind me and turned the horse for home. There, he helped me dismount, and he galloped off. We didn't see him again that night.

The evening after the filming, everyone was flushed with success at what had been achieved. Sergio apparently had been full of praise at the way in which our group had made a realistic habitat for the animals, and the cameraman was sure he had got some excellent and unique footage. I was pleased to hear that, but also sad that I hadn't had the chance to witness the filming.

The feelings of well-being persisted among the men until the next day, and in the morning Peter suggested we should take the day off to visit a nearby extinct volcano. Everywhere you look in the Andes, you can see signs of old volcanos, often topped with snow. You can't help but imagine what it would be like if they suddenly began to erupt, spewing ash over the ancient forests in which we had been trapping. (In fact, in 2015 Volcan Cabulco erupted and many of the areas we trapped, including the Pampa de Sol where Checho and I had rested after hunting for nests, were obliterated by ash.)

It was a glorious, 'glad to be alive' kind of day – with clear blue skies. I felt a little like a kid being given the day off school. The road took us upwards through bald, dry hills which became steeper the higher we climbed. As the road climbed, I could feel the anticipation mounting in my chest. Eventually, the road ran out and we had to leave the *camionetta* and climb the steep sides of the volcano, which was littered with large granite boulders with jagged edges.

From the top, we had a truly spectacular view of the surrounding Andes. To the north, the mountains got higher and appeared different shades of blue. To the south, the mountains looked lower and browner. From our vantage point, we could see rivers of volcanic ash which had made their way down the volcano's slopes, and we could see the *camionetta* parked way down below. Apart from that, there was not a single sign of human existence anywhere. We could have been the only people alive on Earth.

It was hot and still, and we sat down on the boulders to enjoy the view. Eventually, Peter lay back on the rock, and one by one we all joined him. We lay for a while together on the granite, enjoying the fresh clean air, and the powerful warmth of the sun, each using parts of the other as a pillow. I had my head on Peter's chest, Checho and Pedro had their heads on my legs, Peter had his head on Checho's thigh. It was wonderful to realise that we felt comfortable enough with each other to enjoy that level of intimacy.

Eventually, it just felt like it was time to go. Without a word, Checho stood up and ran down the steep mountainside in the river of ash, kicking up clouds of fine dust as he went. I watched him dodge small boulders and slip and slide, and he got smaller and smaller. It looked like fun, but would there be any sinkholes? Might he just disappear from view, sucked up by the volcano's ash? Within seconds, Pedro and Peter had followed suit and I was alone on the top of the volcano. My fear of not being able to find my way walking down alone eclipsed my fear of sinkholes in the ash. I took a running leap off the edge, and fell into the soft grey ash. I quickly realised that in order to breathe one had to keep above the powder clouds. In any case, the volcano side was steep and it was impossible to stop running and remain upright. It was several minutes of an exhilarating obstacle course, taking care not to trip on the many boulders and rocks protruding from the ash. I arrived at the bottom feeling as tired and as exhilarated as if I had run a marathon. I was also proud of myself. I finally felt like I was one of the boys.

Northward bound

A couple of days later, we packed up and headed back to Santiago, taking with us the travelling *monitos*. Peter had organised to pass them onto a local scientist who would continue to observe them in captivity.

Peter had already made plans with Tony that after we had refuelled and organised fresh supplies, we would be going north to a place called Pichidangi, to study *Thylamys elegans*, the elegant fat-tailed mouse opossum, also locally known as *yaca*. I was pleased at the thought of heading north into the warmer parts of Chile.

But it transpired that there was to be quite a big change in the team's line-up.

Just before leaving Puyehue and arriving in Santiago, we had received a 'most urgent' telex, marked as having been sent via the Radio Australia newsroom. John Vandenberg and David Parer of the the Natural History Unit of the Australian Broadcasting Commission in Melbourne had heard that Sergio Nuno was planning to film *monitos* and the shrew opossum, and they wanted some footage too. They asked us to 'beg, borrow or hire a sixteen-millimetre movie camera plus six hundred feet of colour negative film stock from Santiago or elsewhere'. They 'had no hope of getting our American cameraman to the location from his film commitments in Panama. The other alternative is for you to send animals to his location on Barra Colorado Island or Washington Zoo.'

Peter would not consider sending the animals elsewhere and had already promised them to another scientist in Santiago. But he agreed to stay in Santiago for a few days to assist Sergio Nuna with the additional filming and the editing of Sergio's documentary. Lucho was busy too, as he had to package up and send off to various museums the many new species of insects he had collected in Patagonia. Aware that Tony only had another week before he needed to return to Australia, Peter suggested that Tony, Checho and I head on up to Pichidangi, and he and Lucho would join us in a few days. I felt a little disappointed. I would have preferred to stay with Peter, but also realised that Tony would genuinely need my help to communicate with Checho and to manage the traps. While I felt quietly proud that I could make a useful contribution by doing the work of another man, ironically at the end of this next trip I felt as if I had somehow failed as a woman.

This was because we also ended up with two additional 'helpers'. To my surprise, Checho's children, Carolina, eight, and Paulo, six, were in the van as we packed up our gear. I thought perhaps we were to drop them off somewhere en route, although Checho either did not understand my questions about this, or preferred not to say. They were dear little children, who on the journey kept me amused with their songs. These were at once very different and yet similar to Australian nursery rhymes.

> *Dona mercedes se fue a comprar*
> *Una zapatilla de tacon coral*
> *Do re mi fa so*
> *So fa me re do*
> *Do re mi fa so fa me re do-na mercedes se fue a comprar…*

> (Madame Mercedes went to buy
> A coral-heeled shoe
> Do re mi fa so
> So fa me re do
> Do re mi fa so fa me re do)

On the drive up, we passed agricultural land and acres of fruit trees. Women and children stood by the side of the road selling fruit; the enormous peaches tasted absolutely delicious.

As we had not dropped them anywhere, it transpired that the children were staying the night with us. We made camp in a dry and rocky place not far from the beach. A hot wind blew, reminiscent of Patagonia in its ceaselessness, but far less intense. However, it made trapping hard work, as we all sweated copiously clambering up the rocks with the packs of heavy traps.

It wasn't long before the children became tired of us laying the traps. They were hungry and hot and tired. I could see Checho felt harassed, torn between the need to do his work and his responsibility to his children. I felt sorry for him, but also knew there was little I could do to help. The children spoke no English and, while they were very patient with my attempts to speak with them. they clearly saw Tony and me as creatures from another planet. They would not have wanted their father to leave them alone with me.

Eventually, Tony called a halt to the trapping, suggesting we only put half the traps out since only he would be able to properly process any animals we caught. We were all relieved to get back to the campsite and have a snack.

As the afternoon drew on, the wind died, and the sea calmed, and it was lovely to walk along the beach, watching the children dart back and forth between the water and the adults, while singing another song:

> *Negro tu caballo*
> *Blanco tu mochon*
> *Blanca tu sonrisa*
> *y rojo tu corazón*
>
> (Black is your horse
> White is your stump of the olive tree)
> White your smile
> And red is your heart)

The children were really very well behaved, but I remember being struck by the fact that they appeared to have brought no change of clothes, apart from bathers, and they had no jumpers to put on when the sun went down. They had no toothbrushes or toiletry items, but perhaps that was not surprising since we had no water with which to wash. They also had brought absolutely nothing to play with or do, so not surprisingly they really wanted to be with their father the whole time, even when we were checking traps, which did slow the process.

Now that we had no Lucho or Pedro to do the cooking, there was an unspoken assumption that I would take on that task. I was not unhappy about it, although Lucho, who had done the shopping and stocked the van, had very different ideas to mine about staple foods.

The first night we were there, the only recipe I could think of given the ingredients we had was a version of a childhood favourite of mine which I thought the children might like, as it was so bland – apple and tinned tuna in a mild curry sauce with macaroni. It really was pretty tasteless, especially given we had no parsley, which normally gave it some flavour. The children both tasted it and found it revolting, saying it was *muy acido* – too lemony. Checho suggested that I give the children just some plain pasta, but I had mixed it all in together with the sauce. The cardinal rule of keeping pasta separate from all else is known by parents all the world over but, as I was not yet a parent, it just had not occurred to me to save some plain pasta.

I will never forget the look Checho gave me – both withering and pitying. When he asked me what else the children were to eat, I had no idea. I did not realise it was my responsibility to plan their meals too. No one had said anything to me before we left, and I only found out they were coming when they climbed in the van as we drove away from Santiago. I imagined that, as their father, Checho would have had some ideas about what they could eat if they didn't like dinner. It was clear Checho was really cross with me. He whisked the children out of the van where we were eating, and we didn't see him or the children again that night. I have no idea where they went, as the campervan was the only vehicle and we were miles from anywhere. I began to wonder why the children were with us and where they had gone.

I lay awake half the night worrying about the children being hungry.

Now that I am a mother, I can imagine that Checho may have even said to his wife not to worry about the kids going on the field trip with him as there was a woman there who could look after them. While I liked children, and wanted them, I knew very little about them.

Checho and the children reappeared the next afternoon, but he kept them busy playing amongst the rocks and rockpools while Tony and I checked the traps and processed the yaca. When I asked what I could make them all for dinner, Checho replied that they had already eaten. I never found out exactly where they went or what had happened and, in his typical way, Checho refused to be drawn and evaded any questions on the topic. He kept the children busy from then on, and out of Tony's way and mine. I couldn't help but feel I had failed some unknown test he was setting me.

A couple of days later, Peter, Lucho and Pedro arrived in the *camionetta*. Lucho was not surprised to see the children, although Checho was quickly despatched by Lucho to drive them home. I was very happy to see Peter again. We were able to lay twice as many traps. Best of all, Lucho and Pedro took over the cooking and I didn't need to worry about it any longer.

I even had time to lie on the beach one afternoon, where I dozed in the warmth. I could hear the voices of Peter and Pedro and I became aware of a warm weight on me. I imagined Peter had thought I was getting sunburnt and had covered me up with a towel. When I woke up properly, though, a couple of hours later, I could not move my legs. When I looked down, I realised I was covered in sand. Someone had built a twenty-feet-long mermaid tail of sand starting from my waist down.

Pedro told me later that Checho had returned and seen me sleeping on the beach, and suggested that they build the tail together. At the time, I took this as a sign that Checho had forgiven me for being a poor mother-replacement for his children but looking back now, I see it differently. I could not imagine them building a tail on Peter or Tony or Lucho as they slept; they would have seen that as overstepping. Even though I know both Checho and Pedro respected me, their respect for the men was both greater and different.

The thought that I may have found their sand building on my Speedo-clad body to be overly intimate probably did not even cross their minds. But I have often wondered whether Checho would have minded another man building such a tail on his wife's body as she slept. I suspect he would have disapproved.

My other recollections of our time at Pichidangi are hard to pin down. I remember a few events but for some reason the level of detail is not as clear as other parts of the trip. I picture my memories of Pichidangi flying around like insects buzzing around Lucho's blue-ish insect-attracting light. We would sometimes take it in turns dancing beneath the light, trying to catch them with a butterfly net. If only I could scoop up those elusive memories!

Departure

We returned to Santiago, to stay for the last few days with Lucho at Colina. Before we had left on the trip to Patagonia we had stayed in Lucho's house, but this time he suggested we stay in a different, empty but furnished cottage, near his house on the hilltop. There were several houses in Lucho's compound, including one for Checho and his family. Lucho's house was made of concrete and wood. Huge and draughty, it contained rooms dedicated to the preparation and storage of his insect collections. It felt much more like a museum than a home. The wooden cottage we stayed in was decorated with folk art, but while comfortable, I recall all the surfaces being thick with dust. When you sat on the couch or lay your head down on the pillow, clouds of dust would billow up. Even though I was no longer out in the field, I still felt grubby.

We spent days packing up all the field equipment and items we that would not be required in the next few months in London. Tony, who was leaving for Australia just before us leaving for the UK, had agreed to escort the chests to Melbourne and deliver them to Peter's office.

In one tea chest, we packed the ten open wire cages, each packed full of items, duly recorded by me, for example:

Trap 1: faecal pellets, lens mount, I jar of glutaraldehyde (a fixative used in preparation of tissue for electron microscopy, shows far more detail than light microscopy), Nembutal (anaesthetic), two jars of sodium cacolydate (used alongside the glutaraldehyde to help the fixation process).

Trap 2: four medicuts (aspiration or sucking-up syringes, in contrast to injecting syringes), eleven jars of sodium cacolydate, one jar of glutaraldehyde, the rock from Antillanca.

Trap 3: Tony's dirty washing.

Trap 4: tissues in formalin (formalin is a fixative which is used for tissues to be examined using light microscopy).

Another tea chest contained items packed randomly and included a microscope, two boxes of rodent skins, one pair of walking boots, one tripod, three baskets, Tony's sleeping bag, three books, a wooden spoon, one wooden gaucho stirrup, one down jacket, four little dolls, Peter's orange jumper, Peter's and Meredith's waterproof pants, box of rocks.

Peter wanted to work on some of the animal tissue while he was in London, and so it needed to be carried in the hand baggage so that it could be produced with authorising documents at customs. Peter put the glass vials containing the dissected and fixed reproductive tracts and sperm samples, into his carry-on bag. We carefully wrapped each tiny Patagonian opossum bone in tissue, and packed them gently but tightly into a small box, quietly anticipating the pleasure of the staff at the British Museum when we handed them over. The only box which was the right size was one which had previously been used for transporting radioactivity detectors for use in labs, but it fitted nicely into my carry-on bag alongside my diaries and some gifts for my family.

The tea chests (and Tony) were duly farewelled, and I imagined our pleasure at opening them when we finally reached home in the middle of next year.

We had a special last dinner with Lucho, Checho and Pedro at a fancy restaurant, all wearing smart casual clothes. The photos of the event show formal smiles, but I remember how strange we all felt with each other in the unfamiliar context. We seemed so distant from each other, and after we had eaten, no one seemed to want to stay sitting around the dinner table.

On the drive back to Lucho's place, Checho suggested we stop at a dance at the local hall, where apparently some friends of his were keen to meet Peter. When we arrived, it was clear that the locals had been expecting us, and many glasses of alcohol were foisted onto Peter while the women whisked me away to dance. Peter swears that the locals were trying to see how much alcohol he could drink, and given that on previous trips with Lucho and Checho, they, as very light drinkers, had expressed admiration for his capacity for alcohol, perhaps that was the case. I do remember that in forty or so years I have only twice ever seen Peter worse for wear as a result of drinking. One was our wedding night, and this was the other.

Some hours later, when we finally got to bed, and I was sure he was OK, I couldn't sleep. It was our last night in Chile and I didn't want to waste it. Peter was snoring, propped up on pillows. I got up, slipped on a tracksuit and stood on the porch of the cottage and looked around. It was a glorious night. The moon had risen and outside it was still and quiet and almost as bright as early dawn. I could both see and hear the horses in the paddock below moving around. The moon was like a giant light source which was illuminating everything on the hill. I wanted to walk around and look at everything in this interesting light. For the first time in my life, I decided not to let my fear of the unknown stop me. I put on my shoes and went for a walk which circumnavigated the houses on the top of the hill. I didn't feel at all scared. While I was admiring the horses, I suddenly became aware of the sound of footsteps on the road some distance behind me. Once upon a time, such an event would have struck me with terror, but I felt quite calm as I waited to see who it would be.

It was Peter. He had woken up and seen I was not in bed, and was looking for me. I remember wondering if it was first time in that whole Patagonian trip that he had missed me.

The next morning, after loading the *camionetta,* we said stiff and awkward goodbyes to Pedro and Checho, and Checho's family. The closeness we had experienced on the field trip, the sense of being part of a family, was not evident in our farewells. It made me realise that I had had no understanding of the roles or expectations of Araucanian Indians within Spanish culture and the way in which it might affect our interactions once we were back from the field. I was sad as I waved goodbye, knowing it was quite possible that I might never see either of them again.

At the airport, Lucho gave me a quick but genuine hug. Within moments, Peter and I were swept up in the busy-ness of departure with our masses of luggage and Lucho was gone.

Peter and I flew to Rio de Janeiro, where we had a couple of days of relaxing before heading off to London for the next stage of his sabbatical. Despite having travelled around Patagonia under, at times, fairly primitive conditions, neither of us had gotten ill. However, just two days into our Rio trip, we both developed what proved later to be *giardiasis*, a gut infection caused by a microscopic parasite acquired through drinking contaminated water or eating contaminated food.

We both felt a little delicate by the time we headed to Madrid and Paris for a couple of days and then onto London. Little wonder then that our arrival in London on a sunny day seemed like the omen of all good things to come. Perhaps it was why we let our guard down, and left our bags with someone we thought we could trust, at the Institute of Zoology. We did not for a moment consider that he might be distracted or that perhaps he might need to leave his post. I wonder, if after all this time, the doorman remembers the incident at all?

Australia 2016

So I have committed to paper all that I could remember about the trip. But I am still not satisfied. I am tantalised by so many details, seemingly just on the very edge of my memory. It's like an itch that cannot quite be scratched. Where else could I find some answers? I really want to find my diaries. Is there any chance they could be sitting on the bookshelf of someone who found them in Primrose Hill, the day my bag was stolen? Could I really harness the power of social media to help my search?

Like any good detective one sees on TV shows, I decided to collect all the information on the crime that I have to date.

The police record of the theft would be helpful, as I don't recall exactly what the bag looked like, only that it was blue vinyl. Can one just walk into a police station and ask to see an old record, if one was party to reporting the theft? Living in Melbourne, Australia, posed a few challenges for my search. To my surprise, when I googled Camden police station, it became clear that it was possible to email them. Under the heading of Camden Borough, it states,

> You can contact us via email or phone. We will respond to every message directed to us within 4 days. However, we are not an emergency response team, so if it is an emergency, please call 999. If you would like to report a crime, please visit our online crime reporting page.

I filled in my contact details, and ticked the box to confirm that the form is not being used to report something that needs urgent police attention (that is, crime reporting). And then I wrote,

> In January 1986, my then husband and I reported the theft of a

travel bag outside Regent's Park Zoo. I am in the process of writing a book about the contents of this bag (it contained the bones of a small South American marsupial which were destined for the British Museum), and I was wondering whether police reports of that time are still accessible?

Once I pressed send, I immediately got a response that said,

Thank you for writing to your local police. We will endeavour to respond to your email within the next four days.

I took note of the reference number in case I should need to refer back to this communication B01-00081283, and am reminded again that if I require an immediate police response, please call 999.

To my surprise, when I checked my email later that same day (21 February 2016) there was a message which said,

Hello Mrs Temple-Smith
Your email has been forwarded to the relevant unit and they will respond within 7 days
Regards
(Name)
LDSS Camden Borough Team Leader

I was extremely impressed! I immediately felt full of hope that the UK may be organised in ways that Australia isn't, and perhaps my quest might even turn up some evidence!

However, seven days passed, and then another seven, and then after another five days, on 11 March 2016 I sent a reminder.

Dear (Name),
I am following up on your email of 23 February which was in response to my query about whether police reports are still available from 1986. You suggested that someone from Camden Police might respond within 7 days, but as yet I have heard nothing.

(Name) did not let me down again. Three days later, on 14 March, I received a response.

> Hello
>> I do apologise.
>> Police reports are only kept for 7 years then they are destroyed.
>> Regards
>> (Name)
>> LDSS Camden Borough Team Leader

Disappointing. I put the correspondence into a file marked 'Failure'.

Perhaps I might have better luck with the newspaper. A google search revealed that Primrose Hill residents have access to a few local newspapers. The *Ham & High* sounds vaguely familiar, so I tried to find about more about them. They are now owned by Archant Publishers, who seem to own most of the local papers in the UK. I looked on their website and found that they invited readers to submit a story. So on 25 March 2016, I sent via the web (after ticking the box saying that I agreed to the terms and conditions even though the link that opened them led nowhere), the following:

> In January 1986, a local newspaper distributed around Primrose Hill reported a story about the theft of a travel bag from outside Regent's Park Zoo. I am the owner of the bag, and am now in the process of writing a book about its contents (it contained the bones of a small South American marsupial which were destined for the British Museum, along with my diary of the 4 month South American fieldtrip during which the bones were collected). I want to discover the fate of the bones and the diary. A few days after the theft, a member of the public called the zoo and said they had found papers with my name on them in Primrose Hill, but the switchboard operator asked the caller to call back in a few days, and of course that never happened. I wonder if, now, after 30 years, someone (perhaps even the thief?) might be prepared to cast some light on the fate of the bag contents…

After pressing send, I got an immediate response that said,

> Thanks for getting in touch. Thanks for sending us your story. Your message has been passed to our news desk, who will be in touch if

they need any more details. We get dozens of story ideas every day and unfortunately are unable to reply individually to every one- but we always appreciate hearing from our readers.

And when I checked my email, there was a message from the *Ham & High* which said,

Thanks for submitting your story. This is an auto-generated confirmation mail, so please do not reply to this email address.

I hopefully checked my email until the start of May…and then I added this interaction to the Failure File.

I went back online and studied the Google map of Regent's Park Zoo, which clearly shows the building of the Zoological Society of London. It fronts the Outer Circle and at the back and across the other side of the canal, the expanse of the suburb of Primrose Hill is clearly visible. If only I could be there in the flesh, it might trigger so many memories. Suddenly, it seemed the most critical thing to do, to prompt my memory. I needed to go to London!

After our return to Australia from the Patagonian field trip and the time in London, Peter and I had resumed our lives. After the first flurry of welcome by family and friends was over, and we had given a few talks on the trip to interested colleagues, things went back to normal, at least for me. Peter continued to work on different samples he had brought home, and wrote some academic papers. I enrolled in a Master of Public Health degree, worked as a research assistant and concentrated on starting a family. Our eldest daughter joined us in 1988, a son in 1994, and another daughter in 1996. A decade later, Peter and I separated, but we always lived close together, remained good friends and continued to co-parent.

Occasionally over the years, Peter and I had discussed something to do with the loss of the bones, but we didn't ever talk about the details. When I told him about my Failure File, we began to reminisce.

To my surprise, he remembered far more detail about the layout of the Institute of Zoology than me, which, on reflection, was not surprising, as he had been back there a couple of years later. However, he reminded me that while there was a doorman, his glassed-in area was inside the foyer of the building, and not outside, as I had thought, for all these years.

We spent some time laughing about my imagination, and then he went home. A few hours later, he called to say he had found a copy of a letter he had written to his parents on Monday, 17 February 1986, three days after the bag was stolen. It contained a few more details.

We had arrived at Waterloo and called the Institute and then took a taxi over there. Unloaded luggage in the foyer of the meeting rooms and then walked next door to the Nuffield Foundation building to see the director, Dr John Hearn, who was at ANU with me during my PhD, and to meet other people including Dr Harry Moore, who we were to stay with. He gave us his house keys – we went downstairs and the rest is history.

Someone had stolen M's black airline bag from our luggage collection. After the initial shock we started making a mental list of what was inside it (a list which increased in size during the next day.) I guess we were lucky that the irreplaceable fixed material from the marsupials we caught in South America was in my heavy locked bag, but it was painful to realise that M's two diaries, lovingly put together over the last 4 months and our only comprehensive record of the trip, had gone, plus $250 Amex travellers cheques (replaceable), M's Chinese bracelet and some lovely Chilean jewelry, my Argentinean bolas (like three balls attached together with leather thonging), all M's work papers, and sadly, our prized collection of bones from the Patagonian part of the trip which had the largest ever collection of Patagonian opossums' jaws (the rare species we weren't able to catch). We still can't believe our bad luck after so carefully guarding our belongings through South America and then to get ripped off in England. Spent all of Saturday looking around the zoo and Regent's Park and Primrose Hill for the discarded bag – but without luck! Just keeping our fingers crossed that the bag will be dumped intact and some kind person will hand it in.

Wow! On reading this, I could envisage so much more that I had previously forgotten. For a start, I had thought the bag was blue! It was a shock to realise that more of my memories were not as accurate as I had thought. Where on earth did the idea of a doorman's booth come from?

I seriously doubted my memory even more when I was went to London, for work, a few months later.

Early one morning, I took a train to St John's Wood, and then walked to Regent's Park in the cool sunshine. It was very pleasant walking past the mostly white boxy homes with their colourful gardens. The large green trees of Regent's Park created a picturesque backdrop as I walked through the largely empty streets. Crossing over Regent's Canal from Primrose Hill, I stopped to take a photo in both directions.

To my right, several houseboats lined the canal, gently rocking in a breeze which shimmered the water, creating shards of sparkle. To my left, where the canal widened, was the old floating Chinese restaurant, looking dimly mysterious in the long shadows cast by the trees. It all looked vaguely familiar, yet somehow different. On the canal bank on the park side beneath the bridge was lush undergrowth, festooned with litter. I paused and had to fight the temptation to climb down there and crawl through the undergrowth for possible signs of my bag, perhaps discarded over thirty years previously.

I walked over the bridge, turned right and walked twenty metres down the Outer Circle to the Institute of Zoology. From the outside, the building appeared not to have changed at all, but on reaching the front door, it was evident that it was in no way the same. The whole entry was different. Once buzzed in through the security door, the reception area was now to the left, close to the old-style elevator, whose mechanism was on display through black mesh, like in New York movies from the 1940s. I told the sweet-natured receptionist why I was there, but beyond saying that the building had been renovated before she came to work there (and indeed when I was last there, she would not have been born), there was no way she could advise me on what the building had been like before, and everyone who worked there now, she said, was young.

I went outside, looked around a bit more and then began a slow and contemplative walk back to my accommodation in Bloomsbury. I felt strangely let down, but I had no idea why. What was visiting the scene of the crime ever been likely to achieve? We couldn't find the bag when it was newly stolen, so what had I expected? I had no idea.

A few days after my return from the UK, Peter came over for a family dinner carrying a large box. My emailed invitation to dinner had ruefully mentioned my visit to the institute and it had prompted him to search his garage for the photos of the Patagonian trip.

The enormous storage box was packed to the brim with small boxes of slides. I had completely forgotten that Peter had taken many photos of the trip on a good-quality camera. Of course, being a scientist, he did what was considered to provide the best quality shots, and so everything was printed on slide film. I had barely thought of the slides over the last thirty years, as we had never owned a slide projector, although I do remember Peter used to show a handful of slides of the trip at the start of any talks he gave on field trip data.

During dinner, we chatted about a few aspects of the trip. It was so interesting to hear the particular events that held the strongest memories for him. We also had a few good laughs of the kind where one person says, 'Remember…?' And with only a single word, the whole story comes flooding back. I said to the kids that they might find it interesting to read this story, especially those who had been to South America. Having observed us laugh about field trip memories before, Daughter One laughingly expressed concern that it might contain 'TMI' (too much information).

When I was finally alone, I took the lid off the storage box. As I opened the first box, I had butterflies. I held the tiny slides up to the light of my computer screen. The first few appeared to be very good shots of different kinds of trees and shrubs, which I recognised as being those found in Puyehue. After the first couple, I realised that if I was going to look through them, I would need to acquire a slide viewer. Returning them to the box, a couple slipped from the pile, and as I picked them up off the floor I could see flashes of purple and green. I held the slide up to the light and there was me, wearing a very 1970s purple and green tracksuit top I had not even remembered I had! I couldn't wait to source a slide viewer.

A few days later on Sunday morning, the doorbell rang. I was still in bed, putting off the moment when I knew I needed to get up to go to the gym. As I struggled into my dressing gown and down the stairs, I could see through the thin window beside the front door that it was Peter, in his riding gear and with his bike, standing on the other side. As soon as I opened the door, he apologised for the earliness of the hour, even though it was after ten a.m.

As he slowly entered, he said, 'I've come off my bike', but it still took me several moments to realise that he was in pain.

Riding at forty kilometres per hour near the city an hour earlier, his bike had slid on tram tracks, and he had fallen heavily on his shoulder, hip and hand. Despite his attempts to reassure me that all was well and he would be fine to go home after a cup of tea, once I suggested going to the emergency department for some scans, he did not object. Nor did he object when several hours later, I suggested he come to stay with me and the children until his cracked ribs allowed him to breathe without pain.

For me, Peter's accident turned out to be a blessing. For many weeks, I had wanted to ask him his memories of various events but did not want to monopolise family time to do so. Both of us were busy with our own jobs and lives, and I had not wanted to be constantly pecking at him for information. So while he was confined to the comfy armchair in my house, worried about being unable to concentrate on his work, I suggested he might like an activity that would help me but would not require too much effort on his part. He was very happy to read what I had written so far, although when I noticed many scribblings on the pages, I felt a little heart-sink, wondering whether he would disagree with my version of events.

So sometime later, as I retrieved the pages from his sleeping hands,

I was relieved to see that the scribblings were adding details, most of which I had forgotten, to my text. Later, when he woke, he told me how much he had enjoyed reading my words, but also said that it really opened his eyes to how isolated I had felt as the only woman in the group. This trip had been Peter's third time working in the field alongside Lucho and Checho. So the relationships among the men in the group were established, and although Pedro was a newcomer, he was a very junior employee.

Peter acknowledged that Lucho had made an exception to his rule of no women on the field trip for him. The concession, he agreed, had made it imperative for me not to disrupt the usual activity of the field trip in any way. I felt a flicker of pride when he went on to say that I had not caused any major problems, although we both then had a laugh remembering that it was not perhaps exactly true…

On Saturday night, when all the other house occupants were out, Peter and I set up the slide projector I had borrowed. I dragged the large clear storage container filled with assorted boxes of slides into the lounge room. Inside, there were literally hundreds of small slide boxes: long thin yellow boxes with clear lids, smaller oblong boxes with black lids, and orange cubes. Nearly all were marked with a box number, the year and some description of the contents, although later it became clear that not all of the information was accurate. Nonetheless, it was exciting to sort through the boxes, and discovering that here was Box 5, and there was Box 12, and oh, even a Box 26! I even found a Box 55, although in total there were eleven boxes missing. I placed the boxes in order, decanted the contents of the first three, and gave them to Peter to feed into the slide carousel on his lap.

It was truly astounding to see myself, thirty years ago, blown up on the wall, in photos I may have seen once, when they were developed, if at all. I was struck by how unnaturally brown and shiny my face looked, by the incredibly ugly clothing of the 1980s, by the details I had forgotten about the appearance of the campervan and the *camionetta*.

Also in the box with the slides was an archive box of Chilean correspondence. There were many very long and detailed letters from 1985 to 1995 from academics in different parts of the world, commenting on various aspects of the Patagonian trip or on samples which Peter had sent them for their own work. There were letters from a scientist who had been asked to comment on the ticks which had been found in the fur of some animals, there was news of related work or the progress of examinations which was being undertaken on different tissues. This is something I have always admired about zoologists – there is a culture of sharing whatever animal tissue they have amongst others who are researching other body systems.

I was interested to find dozens of telexes and letters from 1985 and 1986 containing interactions with my father, who had managed our finances while we were away. Poor Dad, it must have been a challenge, as we had very little income, and there were tiny amounts of money coming from many different sources that Peter had cobbled together to finance the Patagonian part of the trip.

There was a letter from Tony written on 23 April 1986, telling us of the journey from Santiago to Melbourne with our tea chests. His trip back 'had its exciting moments' with all our luggage being offloaded at Tahiti, and poor Tony needing to argue with Qantas to have the lot taken through to Melbourne at no extra cost.

At Melbourne, his own luggage was last off the plane,

> which was fortunate, for by that time Customs had had enough of inspection. The Inspector took one look at the boxes, asked me what their contents were and waved me through. So I was able to bring the lot to Monash in the car. You should now be able to walk around Victoria in your boots and contaminate the entire state with Foot and Mouth.

He also reported that the footage we obtained for the ABC was good and they were happy with it.

A letter from my mother dated 3 February 1986 said,

> We were so sorry to hear about your bag, what rotten luck. You

must feel like murdering the thief – especially since the contents would be of little use to anyone.

I found another letter to my parents, written a few days before we left the UK in 1986, where I reported that I had had *another* bag stolen in London.

I did a contemporary dance class, which I really enjoyed. I took my handbag up to the studio but left my tracksuit, underpants, bra and a jumper in a bigger bag with my shoes and socks… While I was dancing, I had a moment of doubt – I was sure the bag was calling me! Of course it was no surprise to find it gone on my return. My initial upset was directed at the loss of the bag rather than its contents, until I realised I had very little to put over my tights to meet Peter and some friends in an Indian restaurant! Fortunately my raincoat wasn't taken so I could wear that. Naturally I reported the theft to the security people (I couldn't go to the police, my map of London having been stolen). I didn't enjoy the meal with the friends at all, and when we got home we were told that someone had called to say they'd found the bag barely five minutes after I had left the studio. So I got it back the next day, completely intact. It had been stuffed down behind a toilet at the dance school. Stolen bags were high on the agenda last week because we also went to the British Museum of Natural History, behind the scenes, to visit the only 6 specimens ever to have been caught of the Patagonian opossum. It was heart wrenching to find the jawbones there EXACTLY matched both P's and my memories of our stolen jawbones. However, good also, because if we can manage to retrace our steps in Argentina we may have luck in finding them again. It was interesting there behind the scenes, we also saw the original specimen of the playtpus (the first one ever sent to the UK) in 1794 – I held it in my hands…it was only a baby.

In one letter, written just before we returned to Australia in 1986, my mother commented that they had received several boxes of developed slides of the Patagonian trip, and they had looked through them, and found them 'very nice'. The distant politeness of this tone was not what either of us expected – I thought my parents would have been so interested and excited to see the slides, and said so. When I said this to Peter, he asked me whether the boxes of slides included photos of me in the hotel in Buenos Aires. In the next letter I wrote to my parents, I included the conversation I had had with him which went like this:

Peter: Did those slides include photos of you in the hotel in Buenos Aires?

Meredith: I didn't know you'd taken a photo of me there.

Peter: You don't know lots of places I've taken photos of you!

Meredith: Like where for example?

Peter: Not telling… [Eventually, after a lot of pushing.] Well, you were asleep in the hotel in Buenos Aires. You looked so nice lying on the bed with no clothes on and the sunlight streaming through the blinds onto you.

Meredith: What do you mean by no clothes on?

Peter: Naked.

Meredith: What! Naked! Why did you take a photo?

Peter: Don't be upset. I don't think you'll be disappointed!

Meredith: That's not the point! What were you going to do with them?

Peter: Oh. I hadn't thought about that.

When I eventually saw the slides some months later, I had to agree that the dappled light did make an attractive pattern on my body. However, the artistry of the slide was somewhat ruined by the fact that I was clearly dead to the world, with my mouth wide open!

At the time, I was upset by this but I wasn't sure why. I didn't really care about my parents seeing me naked, as they had watched me perform as a dancer wearing very body-hugging clothing on many occasions. Now, I recognise that I felt objectified. I can't imagine taking a photo of someone else, male or female, who was asleep and naked, without telling them. By today's standards, it is likely to be seen as a highly intrusive act, yet I know it wasn't really intended that way. But that was what life was like in those days.

There were also many letters in Spanish from Lucho, often containing a note from Checho, always sending *un abrazo* (a hug) for Peter and *un beso* (a kiss) for Meredith.

Lucho had, in fact, died many years before, in September 1995, at the age of seventy-four. I was aware that early in the millennium a whole new genus of beetles bore his name, *Luchoelmus*. The authors of the paper announcing the *Luchoelmus* genus stated the etymology of the name as

> Lucho (Luis) Pena plus elmis. Lucho was a friend, an entomologist, conservationist, and author of numerous books and scientific articles concerned with Chilean natural history subjects (Spangler and Staines, 2002).

Lucho had been described after his death as 'the last Chilean naturalist' because of his broad interests and knowledge (Larrain 2008). He had discovered and named over four hundred species of beetles. Over his lifetime it was said that he made more than five hundred expeditions, exploring insects, birds, animals and plants. He was also acknowledged as an excellent science communicator, bringing the natural world alive to children through his contributions to the popular Chilean children's comic *Mamputo*. He also was credited with overseeing the scientific quality of several natural history TV series. Lucho's commitment to his work lives on in his nephew, Alfredo Ugarte Pena, who now lives in Colina and has become a well-known TV personality because of his commitment to insects.

Peter had acknowledged Lucho in one of his papers which arose from the South American trip (Frankham and Temple-Smith, 2012). And he also acknowledged me…

> This paper is dedicated to the memory of Luis (Lucho) Peña Guzman (1921–1995). The *Dromiciops* specimens used in this study were obtained under a permit from Corporacion Nacional Forestal de Chile (CONAF) to L.P. Guzman. We acknowledge the field assistance of M. Temple-Smith, D. Taggart, J. (Checho) Escobar, P. Salinas, and the advice and assistance of J. Rottman (CONAF). We also acknowledge the help and support of local Araucanos fam-

ilies at Lago Chapo who provided accommodation and field assistance for the project. L.P. Guzman (deceased) is gratefully acknowledged for his friendship, organizational skills, assistance with fieldwork, permits, and planning, and his broad knowledge of the natural history of Chile.

When I first read this, I remember a flash of pride at my acknowledgement for 'field assistance'. But I also recall speculating that the acknowledgement in no way could ever reflect the effort and commitment involved. For David and Tony, the field trip formed part of their work and contributed to their career development (David) or to a capstone pre-retirement project (Tony). Lucho, Checho and Pedro were also paid, and the families at Lago Chapo were paid for our food and camping spot. So what did I earn from the trip?

When I first met Peter, and visited his office, I was shocked by the piles of paper. It looked as if nothing had been filed for years. One of our early 'dates' was at his office, with him preparing a lecture, while I (at my suggestion) labelled and filed a vast amount of paperwork. I felt thrilled to be able to contribute something to help his academic life; I hoped that I would absorb the knowledge or ideas in his papers. I wanted not only to become more connected to him by understanding what he did, but also to have him realise I could be useful. When I had finished, his office looked tidy and welcoming (a situation which lasted about a week).

At the time, I wondered how he ever kept his thoughts in order, if he couldn't keep his office tidy. But in some ways, that messy office also contributed to my view of him as an intellectual whose brainpower far outstripped mine. We both recall in the early stages of our relationship that I expressed surprise that he, a rising academic, would be interested in me. I felt like an unformed being in comparison to him. He is seven years older than me, but since a child he had always known what he wanted as a career, and single-mindedly pursued it. I wanted him to be proud of me, and his colleagues to be impressed by me, and I saw myself as having limited academic ability. I hoped that my playing some kind of part in his fieldwork would give me respect from his colleagues.

Now that I am a professor, this self-perception of my ability probably seems ridiculous, but it was not without cause. Until Year 11, I had been an excellent student at the five different schools I attended in Melbourne, Brisbane and Sydney. The changes were made as my father was often transferred within his company. But in the final two years of yet another new secondary school, back in Melbourne, I really struggled.

I had been encouraged by the new school to study 'hard' sciences – chemistry, maths and physics – as so few girls opted for those subjects. I found it challenging at the age of fifteen to break into any of the established friendship groups at my new school. I joined extracurricular groups – athletics, choir, plays, the community welfare group, the school dance committee. I tried so hard to belong. While I eventually found a group of friends and a best friend, I did not do as well in my final exams as everyone expected, including me.

As soon as my exams were over, we moved to Johannesburg for my father's work, so once again I was again in a setting where everything was foreign. This was especially different, though, as in the early 1970s, South Africa was still in the grip of apartheid. Under the guise of freedom to develop at their own pace, laws forced the different racial groups to live separately, and any social integration between groups was forbidden.

For a girl like me who had grown up in a safe environment, life in South Africa was outside my comprehension. I had barely begun at the University of Witwatersrand when there was a demonstration on campus to commemorate the Sharpeville massacre, an event in 1960 where police had opened fire on black protestors, killing sixty-nine and wounding a hundred and eighty. Until the late 1960s, opposition to apartheid had been led by white university students, but in 1969 a black medical student named Steve Biko led a breakaway group called the South African Students Organisation, and many of the demonstrations I witnessed on campus were led by the group. As Steve Biko grew in popularity, he became increasingly dangerous to the government, until he was banned and detained without charge in 1973. Eventually he was imprisoned and tortured, and died in custody in 1977.

In 1972, the year I was there, I witnessed events I had previously only seen in movies. One day, I remember trying to walk into the main gates of the university where many students were demonstrating with placards and banners. Police arrived to break it up, and I saw a policeman use his truncheon to hit a girl in a wheelchair until he toppled her over. I have always felt ashamed that I didn't go to her assistance, but I was terrified and ran as fast as I could through the gates to what I thought was the safety of the campus.

An hour later, though, in my chemistry lecture, we all became aware of an acrid smell and our eyes began to water. Recognising it was tear gas, the lecturer told us to quickly get out of the lecture theatre. As people began to exit the front doors, they ran into clusters of police who were waiting to arrest any demonstrators they recognised who may have been hiding among us. They seemed to be grabbing anyone at random. Over their screams of protest, a boy I didn't know yelled to follow him, and several of us ran up the stairs at the back of the theatre which looked as if they led only to the projection room. The exit opened onto a landing shared by the exits of a few lecture theatres, and we were able to escape by entering the back door of an empty theatre, running down the steps to ground level and exiting through the front door, which was a little distance away from the action.

I downplayed this event to my parents as I didn't want them to worry when I auditioned for the University Players and got a minuscule part in the chorus of a play called *Emperor Bolly, or when the balloon went up*. Based on the childhood tale, 'The Emperor's New Clothes', it was a thinly disguised commentary on apartheid. The lead in the play was Jonathon Paton, an English lecturer and the son of Alan Paton, well-known South African anti-apartheid activist and renowned author of many books, including *Cry, the Beloved Country*. On opening night, Jonathon was arrested by the police, who wanted the play to be cancelled. But in time-honoured tradition, the play had to go on, and someone else stepped in to play the lead. I was thrilled to end up with a small speaking part. My parents were not so thrilled, and in fact were increasingly worried that my behaviour was going to lead to some serious problems. As it turned out, they had good reason for concern.

All residents of Johannesburg were white, apart from live-in housekeepers or maids. All people of colour were required to live in townships outside the city and commute to work each day. These racial segregation laws made no sense to me and I had no idea of the consequences of ignoring them until a single terrifying event.

My Japanese university biology tutor was classified as an 'Honorary White', a situation which I believe resulted from trade agreements between South Africa and Japan. He invited me to go to a party with a white law student friend. I was very excited to go, as I think it may have been the first time I had been asked to any social event outside the family. I was collected from my home by the law student and my tutor, who sat in the back of the car. We then drove to a nearby township to collect my tutor's girlfriend, who, as Chinese, was classified as non-white, and thus prohibited from living in Johannesburg.

It was the first time I had been to a township and I was shocked to see the humble homes, the poor street lighting and the absence of shops and amenities. We collected the young lady and quickly left the township. A few minutes later, on a stretch of road with no street lighting, between the township and the outskirts of Johannesburg, we were pulled over by two police vans. As several policemen emerged from the back of each van, with flashlights and truncheons, the law student swore and then told us all to lock the car doors.

Without even attempting to talk to us, the police surrounded the car and used their combined weight to rock the car from side to side, while they hit the car with their truncheons and yelled at the tops of their voices. It was an action designed to terrify and it worked. Eventually, the law student rolled the window down an inch and spoke to the policeman in charge, who claimed we were contravening the Immorality Act, and wanted us to go with them in the van.

The law student cleverly countered by stating that I was the daughter of the Australian ambassador, and that the situation would create a diplomatic incident. The police took the couple in the back into one of the vans, and the other van escorted us home. The student then went back with the police. I never saw him again, and I am not sure I ever even knew anything other than his first name, but I am so grateful to him. Apparently, my tutor and his girlfriend were held without questioning for days, and then released with a warning. I only ever saw my tutor once more, when he invigilated at an exam I was sitting. As soon as possible, my parents sent me back to Australia.

I was relieved in some ways. In Johannesburg, while I had met some interesting people, it could be frightening to find yourself to be the only white in certain parts of town. Completely justifiable resentment could be seen in the eyes of some black passers-by. With the arrogant ignorance of one who had no real understanding such matters, I had once entered a shop through the 'blacks only' entrance and was memorably and quite rightly told off by a nearby black shopper. It was a good lesson to not take my white privilege for granted.

Recently, I came across a sheet of 1972 final first year results for myself and others, which, as was common in pre-internet days, had been posted publicly on the university noticeboard. There are eight names listed on the page with surnames starting with Su to To (Sullivan to Toner), and each person had attempted four subjects. I had passed one subject (biology) and failed three subjects (chemistry, maths and physics), and thus had failed the year overall.

But what surprises me now is that, in total, five people listed on that page had failed. While it is possible that every other page may have shown the majority of people to have passed, I can't help but wonder now whether the significant disruptions to campus life from the constant anti-apartheid demonstrations within and outside the university had affected us all badly.

So my second attempt at first year university was at Monash University, where I was living in the halls of residence. Through my thespian interests – this time performing in the Halls Revue, I met some dancers from the Monash Modern Dance Group. They suggested I come to dance classes, which soon became the highlight of my days. I began with Afro-Cuban dance, and added jazz ballet, and occasionally tap. Soon, I was spending as much as twenty hours each week taking dance classes and practising for performances, and also spending far too many hours working at the local milk bar (for the princely sum of a dollar an hour) to earn the money to pay for classes.

No wonder I failed two more subjects, although I conveniently became quite ill just before the exams. Given I had no relatives nearby, the university sent me off to Fairfield Hospital, where there was great excitement when it was revealed that I had recently spent time in Africa. Countless medical students came in to prod my mind and body, and I think there was great disappointment all around when a diagnosis of glandular fever was made. I was very relieved to be discharged, though, as I had been in a two-bed locked ward. The other occupant was a fourteen-year-old girl from a girls' home, who had slashed a taxi driver's throat with a broken bottle. Or maybe she just told me that to scare me into letting her hide in my belongings a cigarette lighter she had stolen from a doctor. I was too frightened to go to sleep in case she set the ward on fire.

My family eventually returned to Australia in 1974 and I moved back with them. In my entire science degree, however, the highest mark I ever got was a credit for physiology in second year.

With that academic record, it was no surprise that I saw Peter as an intellectual giant and myself as someone with limited career prospects. I did enjoy my work as a research assistant, which I began when I was completing third year as an undergraduate and was employed by the academic who had a thing for girls with long blonde hair.

Academia then was littered with often young, capable women who become the right hand of senior male, and nowadays sometimes female, academic staff. The role could be compared to that of a personal assistant, someone who is efficient and knowledgeable and shores up the career of the employer, often at the expense of developing their own career. I had several such roles in my research assistant days.

Some senior staff are good at acknowledging their assistants in such roles, and I am sincerely grateful that the second academic I worked for included me as author on all of his papers where I contributed to his work. Many others are not so generous. However, this early work gave me a great deal of experience in the rudiments of research while allowing me the flexibility I wanted to pursue my passion for dance. I subsequently continued working as a research assistant for several years in different universities while completing two post-graduate diplomas.

I did a Diploma in Applied Child Psychology, thinking I might be a child psychologist. The first three clients, all under the age of ten, showed me that it was the family and not the children who needed help. I felt completely out of my depth and decided that job was not for me. I went in another direction entirely and did a Diploma in Movement and Dance, which offered the potential for work as a dance therapist. But while I loved the study of dance theory, my interest was in choreography and performance, and I suspected that I did not have the self-discipline needed for what I saw then to be the long-term physical demands of the job.

Together, now, I see these diplomas both as acknowledging some of my strengths but representing the confusion I felt about my future. My mother once said to me that she didn't mind what I did with my life, as long as I didn't go into anything to do with the mind or choose a career on the stage. It's fascinating to me now that I was always lured by both. Was it simply defiance then that attracted me to those topics? In any case, I did pretty well in both, but while they both helped to redeem my belief in my ability to succeed in study, I wasn't sure about their legitimacy in the eyes of others. Fitting in was so important to me.

Following Patagonia, while Peter was working at Regent's Park Zoo in London, I was lucky enough to get a few months' work at St Thomas' Hospital as a research assistant. It contributed to a growing interest in community medicine, as it was called back then, and on our return from overseas, I decided I wanted to complete a Master of Public Health degree, at Monash University. In those days, it was taught at the Alfred Hospital, and only open to those who had completed a medical degree. I was determined to get in, and eventually succeeded. Soon after, the degree became available to anyone with an interest in public health. I excelled in the coursework and, for the first time, my abilities suddenly aligned with an interest in something I now saw as a 'legitimate' career.

It wasn't long before I began to see I had something I could offer to the academic world for which I also felt some passion. The world was then abuzz with a new pandemic – HIV. The disease, like all sexually transmissible infections, needed researchers interested in both the clinical and the psychological – a perfect mix for me! This marked the start of my journey as a researcher in sexual and reproductive health.

Several years later, I did my doctoral degree part-time, with most of the work completed at night or at weekends. As a mature-age student, with a decade of specialised topic knowledge, great academic networks and years of experience of managing other people's research, it was not as difficult as most people imagine.

Inside my dad's wallet, after he died, I found he had handwritten a quote from Calvin Coolidge, the thirtieth US president from 1923 to 1929.

> Nothing in the world can take the place of persistence. Talent will not. Nothing is more common than unsuccessful men of talent. Unrewarded genius is almost a proverb. Education will not. The world is full of education derelicts. Persistence and determination are omnipotent.

I had never known that was how my dad felt, yet I am sure I learnt it by osmosis. Neither of my parents had completed secondary school. Dad left school at thirteen years old after sitting for the Queensland Post Office exam in the 1930s. He delivered telegrams, became a telegraph operator, and then joined the navy when he was eighteen.

Mum had wanted to do nursing or medicine. She was sitting in class in Kerang High School in rural Victoria when the local dentist came into the class and said he needed an apprentice dental nurse. Interested girls were asked to raise their hands. Mum sat on her hands, as she wanted to finish school and go to university. But the teacher ignored all of the girls with their hands up, and told fourteen-year-old Mum that she had to go now with the dentist. That was her last day of school. Ultimately she, too, joined the navy when she was eighteen. When I think now about the limits of my parents' schooling, I am so proud of them and all they achieved. Their curiosity, resilience and interest in new experiences rubbed off on all of their children, and for that I am really grateful.

Motherhood had always been an important goal for me, and many times during the Patagonian trip I had been made aware of how unusual it was in Chile for a woman of thirty, my age at the time, to be childless. It was not through lack of trying before the trip. Peter and I both had been aware of children overseas in need of families. I remember being impressed when I met him that Peter had a 'foster' child he funded through UNICEF.

When I was young, I had endless fantasies of working in Africa with sick babies, although I have no idea of what might have put that in my head. I even had pictures of African babies (alongside a softly draped blue dress which I fancied as a wedding dress) on my bedroom desk for years.

Before we married, Peter and I had discussed the idea of making a family by adoption. But once we were married, under the regulations at that time, we found we would need to wait for four years before we could apply to adopt. That seemed a long time, and to fill it we decided to make one child naturally. I had hoped that Patagonia might work some magic in this regard, but there was almost no opportunity to try. Once we had started the field trip, work was the focus. And truthfully, while on the road, the lack of privacy, combined with being cold and exhausted and grubby all the time, drove any thoughts of procreation from my mind. On the odd occasion we slept in proper accommodation, I was busy luxuriating in the warm water and clean bed linen while

Peter was busy luxuriating in the intellectual equivalent with other academics. Making a baby was a back-up plan after all.

On our return to Australia, after several early pregnancy losses and failed IVF, ultimately genetic testing made it clear that pregnancy would be impossibly complex. And frustratingly having achieved the mandatory four years of marriage, changes in regulations around inter-country adoption complicated and further delayed the quest for parenthood.

Eventually, in the late 1980s, we were successful, and I was lucky to be a stay-at-home mother to our three children for many years.

I was reminded of how important motherhood is to my self-esteem when, after my mother's death, my father found a card I had written to her, many years earlier.

I loved being a stay-at-home mother, but it did have some downsides. At a time when more and more women were working outside the home and childcare was becoming more available, I recall feeling looked down upon by women who worked. Many of Peter's academic colleagues were women or had wives who were also academic, and once again I felt on the outer among them. I was both amused and annoyed by one academic couple to whose place we were regularly invited, along with many other academic families. The children and Peter would be welcomed by the hostess and sent off to play, or talk to the other guests, while my help would immediately be required in the kitchen. It seemed that the working status of the other women and the men present either precluded or excused them from assisting. This pattern was so marked it became something of standing joke between Peter and me.

Certainly having only one income in an increasingly consumer-driven world was challenging, but neither Peter nor I were concerned with keeping up with the Joneses. We both have a 'make-do' mentality. On a broader level, I think this attitude of trying to make the best of things has not always served me or those around me well, and I can see now that there have been times when I would have been better to have forged a new path, or replaced an item, process or even person that didn't work well for me rather than to continue down the same old track.

I didn't work until our eldest daughter commenced school, and then I worked a very small fraction of full-time until our son joined the family. I had just commenced work one day a week during his kindergarten hours, when news of Daughter Two arrived, and my then boss and academic mentor suggested I resign and instead consider undertaking a part-time doctorate. She herself had done so when her children were small. Despite my initial horror that such a feat would be beyond me, it proved to be fantastic advice.

My parents and extended family provided all kinds of help when I was completing my thesis. My mother, for example, would drive with me to the clinics where I interviewed the doctors who were the subjects in my research (the role of the GP in the control of sexually transmissible infections) and she would take the younger children to a nearby park while I did the interviews. We'd have a picnic lunch and then drive home. The children recycled my scrap paper to make little books, and I only remember one incident when Daughter Two helpfully 'decorated' (obliterated all the writing on) my work, which meant I needed to start some of my data analysis again.

I eventually received my doctorate in 2001, when my children were thirteen, seven and five, and I was in my forties. At the afternoon tea after the graduation ceremony, a stranger told me she had been sitting behind my children who were in the audience with their father and grandparents. When she congratulated me on their good behaviour throughout the ceremony, I nearly burst with pride. In fact, it's true to say I got a greater thrill from that than being handed the degree.

There is no doubt in my mind that travelling alone with men and exposure to the Araucano families in Chile had stimulated my interest in the psychosocial aspects of health research. My research, my life interests in sensitive issues and marginalised populations, I am sure comes from my experiences of living and travelling overseas. There is nothing like living among strangers in a different country to make you realise how easy it is for others to misjudge you and, similarly, how you may misjudge others.

I have had, in Chile, Spain and France, people raise their voices and even yell at me in the hopes that it would improve my ability to understand what they were saying, when the issue was simply that my ability to speak their language was limited. I do know what it is like to be uncertain that you are doing the right thing, when you are hoping to fit in.

In Patagonia, which was the pre-children stage of life for me, it had not struck me that most people love and want the best for their children, no matter their status in life and where they are in the world. I have watched families eat together in local restaurants in cities like Dubai, Hong Kong and Seoul, and in rural Australia, Chile and Africa. I have mused over the fact that in every family of three children there seems to be a restless child, a fussy eater and a compliant child, often overseen by a hawk-eyed grandparent, a tired mother and a father who doesn't notice what the kids are doing. Feeding children is something that binds parents and grandparents together across the world.

My interest in different cultures was likely initiated and definitely reinforced by my father. My first recollection of being proud of his knowledge of other cultures was in 1960, when I was six. Our family didn't have a TV, but we had friends who regularly watched the variety show *In Melbourne Tonight*. Each episode, a letter was drawn from a barrel to choose a person to go into the studio for the next episode. They would spin a giant wheel for a prize, which they could win by correctly answering a general knowledge question.

There was great excitement in the house when we heard that someone had nominated Dad for a spot on *The Wheel*, even though at that age I had no idea what it meant. My sister and I went into the neighbour's house for the evening and I slept on their couch until they woke me so I could see my mum sitting in the studio audience and my dad spinning the wheel. The question, asked by a very youthful Bert Newton, was 'Who is the Emperor of Ethiopia?' The audience was quiet. To the amazement of everyone, Dad correctly answered Haile Selassie. The applause from the audience seemed to go on forever!

I heard my parents recount that story many times over my life. Always, the listening party would express astonishment that Dad would know the answer to that question, and each time I would experience a twinge of pride. Dad's prize was an electric typewriter (which he sold) and fifty pounds worth of goods from the Darrod's Department Store. The family outing to spend the money was such an event! A young woman met us at the store entrance and escorted us around. The first thing we bought was bathers for my baby brother. They were white with blue edging and had the words 'L'il lifesaver' in red on the bottom.

I was always curious about different cultures. I started school at five and my first ever birthday party was my sixth. I was allowed to invite five girls, as, customary with parties at the time, the number of guests was calculated as the age of the birthday child minus one. One of the girls I invited was an Aboriginal girl who was in my class at school for a term and then disappeared. She either spoke no English or was too scared to speak, but I loved her smooth dark skin, her stillness and the way she observed things. She and her older sister were living with an older white couple (they looked like grandparents to me). I still have the present she brought to the party, a book titled *Jesus loves you*.

The other special friend I had made at school was a little boy who wore black velvet shorts with braces and a frilly white shirt, and who also spoke no English. His family lived in the nearby migrant hostel, and although I didn't invite him to my party, a birthday card from him appeared in my letter box with an unprocessed stamp in the bottom left-hand corner. It had a picture of a baby in a pram on the front, over the words *Glad you are having a baby*. Inside was a single painstakingly written word – his name: Vincent. I recall my parents were impressed by the effort an adult had made on his behalf to deliver the card to our address, and that they asked me lots of questions about how we became friends, the answer to which I have long since forgotten.

One of my favourite childhood books was *Away Goes Sooty*. Sooty is a little black dog whose clothing matches the unnamed European countries he passes through as he searches for a dear little (white) cat, named, if you can believe it, Bimbo. Naturally, Bimbo is finally found at the farm where the farmer's wife had first noticed her missing (she didn't seem to have looked too hard to find her). While I loved imagining the travels depicted in the Sooty book, I was even more excited when my father brought home for me *Life in Pakistan*, which was a realistic outline of the daily life of a boy about my age, his daily routine, what he ate and where he prayed. My imagination ran wild. I couldn't wait to be able to travel!

I still have in my possession a school project I completed in primary school on Japan. I can clearly remember my mother helping me to put a few grains of rice into a cellophane bag and paste it in the project book as an illustration. Fortunately, unlike my schoolfriends who grew up on meat and three vegetables for dinner, we ate rice a lot. The moment Mum bought her Sunbeam electric frypan, I don't recall her ever again cooking anything typical for an Australian family in the early 1960s. She hated the whole idea of cooking and determinedly aimed for, and consistently achieved, a one-pot dinner – Japanese sukiyaki and Spanish-flavoured rice-a-riso were two regulars.

As the export manager for an Australian company, my dad spent three-quarters of every year travelling overseas, finding new markets for Australian products. After he died, I found a card that I had written to him, telling him how grateful I was for his storytelling of his interactions with people of different cultures, and his unfailing ability to treat everyone the same, from a cleaning lady to a queen (and he had met both!). I am sure it contributed to my interest in and strong sense of connectedness to people from other parts of the world.

Unusually, when I had needed to go to boarding school in Sydney to prevent another disruption to my education when the family moved to Melbourne, my father selected one that had many Asian boarders. I recall him saying that Australia's economic future would be tied up with Asia, and I should learn to be friends with some Asian girls. He also, uncommonly for the time, employed an Asian secretary. This attitude, shared by Mum, definitely normalised the value of ethnic diversity.

Cultural diversity of a different kind came in the slightly pretentious but wonderfully exotic form of one of my mother's many sisters, who was married to a communist playright and lived in Sydney. When I was fourteen, her husband couldn't use his ticket to a new musical, which happened to be on the Friday night of the one weekend boarders were allowed to stay with relatives. My aunt, who was both childless and clueless when it came to children, collected me from school, unplaited my hair and put lipstick on me, and then took me into a club with my school uniform hidden by her voluminous coat.

We then went to see *Hair*, a rock musical made famous by its on-stage nudity. In the middle of the show, she said to me in a loud voice, 'Let me know if you don't understand anything, darling. You do know what fuck means, don't you?' Of course, I said yes, and, of course, I had no idea. Not even a vague one. At the end of the show, the audience was invited to come up to dance on the stage with the cast, and my aunty sent me up there, in my school uniform. I couldn't wait to get back to school on Sunday to ask someone what fuck meant. I was only brave enough to ask one girl. She said it was when a grown-up man sucked on a woman's breast. I spent several years being confused whenever I heard that word, and it was years before I learnt I was working with the wrong definition!

If Dad ever was overseas for the birthdays of one of his kids, he would send a telegram written in the language of the country he was in. He always brought us home little trinkets which are available in airports everywhere these days but were not quite so common in the 1960s and 1970s. I still have a coconut 'box' with a metal clasp from Samoa, strings of beads from various African countries, a little head with feathers attached made from a carved nut from New Guinea, a Japanese doll, and a brass pot from the Middle East, all now over fifty years old. (In those days, Australian Customs was clearly far less fussy about the introduction of plant and animal products.)

We could hardly wait for Dad to return from wherever he was to hear his latest stories. He travelled in the Middle East to Riyadh, sitting next to a man with a hooded falcon on his arm. He travelled in tiny aircraft on the milk run in New Guinea, selling buckets to rubber plantation owners, and saw a woman breast feeding a piglet. He'd been on the Concorde, an aircraft so skinny that many of the controls in the cockpit were on the side of the plane as well as at the front. We loved to hear descriptions of the food he'd eaten and the hotels where he had stayed. Towards the end of his travels, he began to collect beer coasters and swizzle sticks and always there was loose change around the house in every imaginable currency. He passed the travel bug onto all three of his children and all of his grandchildren.

Once Dad was away, we didn't hear from him. He sometimes tried to call but difficulty in connection, the cost and the long delays meant you could have only the most rudimentary conversation. We knew we could send a telex if there was an emergency, but Mum said she'd rather not talk than have a meaningless conversation.

I think Mum longed for a normal marriage. Friends would invite her out or to go their dinner parties, but she often refused because women rarely went alone to anything in those days and she hated to be the odd one out. Dad's absences also meant she often ended up having to turn her hand to the odd jobs other people's husbands would do. She was like a pioneer woman to me, and I wanted her knowledge and self-sufficiency. Even though she always deferred to Dad as the ultimate authority – 'Your father thinks…' – we kids all believed that, by default if not choice, she wore the pants in the household.

So our household was mostly female…my mother, my sister who is five years older than me, and a brother six years younger. My sister spent time away from the family at a different boarding school, at nursing school and then overseas, so her presence was intermittent.

And with four of my six schools being all girls' schools, I grew up with very little exposure to boys or men. I also grew up with a very traditional view of men's and women's roles, despite my mother's self-sufficiency. This probably comes from growing up as a girl in the 1950s. In the early 1960s, I joined the Brownies in the hope that one day I might become a Girl Guide. I notice that my Brownies recruit card states that a Brownie must know the law, the salute, the smile, the good turn. Also given equal billing on the list is 'How to fold her own tie' and 'How to wash up the tea things'. I am pretty sure the Cubs, the junior version of the Boy Scouts, did not include housework as essential knowledge.

To me, boys, and indeed men, were quite a mystery, and I am periodically shocked at how little I knew of them. A good example is this. In my final year of school, I was given a part in a play which was being performed with a local boys' school. The play was called *The Lady's not for Burning* by Christopher Fry, set in the 1400s, about religion and witchery. I played the ingenue, Alizon Elliot, a role played in London in 1949 by Claire Bloom, opposite the great actor Richard Burton.

I loved the complex language of the play even though, at sixteen, I probably didn't understand it the way I do today. For example, 'Men are strange. It's almost unexpected to find they speak English' and 'Show me daffodils happening to a man!' There was great excitement among the cast, as the play called for a stage kiss between me and Richard (an orphaned clerk). At the first rehearsal of the kiss, the drama coach explained in some detail how we needed to stand. Alizon (me) was to face the audience, and Richard stood in profile. I was to have my upstage hand on his shoulder, and my downstage hand flat on the front of his hip. We spent some time in this position, and I noticed Richard seemed a little uncomfortable.

When I came home from rehearsal, I found my parents had friends over for dinner. In the kitchen, Mum asked me how rehearsal had gone, and I told her I was worried about the kiss, because Richard seemed uncomfortable. I felt where I was touching his hip I could feel something like the end of a roll of fat. I asked her if I should ask him about it. She asked me to show her how we stood, and then said very seriously that she thought I would be best not to mention it to him, but that I should try to avoid touching it.

A few minutes later, from the dining room, I heard a collective burst of laughter, and even though I had not heard the preceding conversation, I had the impression that they were laughing about me. I had no idea why. It was years before I realised that Richard had had an erection. I can't believe how ignorant I was. At sixteen, I genuinely did not know men could get an erection with their clothes on. I just thought that was something that happened when people decided to make a baby! (Perhaps this anecdote offers some insight into how I ended up as a sexual health researcher.)

If ever I found myself in an unfamiliar situation with the opposite sex, I would never be brave enough to speak up. I would pretend to feel comfortable even if I was dying inside. In Year 12, I went to a school dance with a boy whose father collected us after the event. The three of us sat in the front bench seat in the car on the way home with me in the middle. While his father stoically concentrated on driving, the boy put one arm around my shoulders and his hand up my skirt, and kissed me very enthusiastically. Every time I tried to squirm away, I would feel the father's body against me, and I remember the horrible feeling of being trapped. I had no idea of how to stop it, even though I knew both the boy and the father to be nice people.

The ultimate example of my sixteen-year-old compliance was when a man in his mid-twenties with whom I had had a single conversation, and whom I knew through school, appeared one Saturday at our door and asked to speak to my mother. A half an hour later, she called me in and told me that he would like to take me on a date. She was clearly happy about it and, while she gave me the opportunity to say no, I felt as if I should say yes.

We went to a restaurant for dinner, and during dessert he suggested I stop calling him 'Mr H...' and instead call him by his first name. In the following few months, we continued to date. He always sought my mother's approval of the places we went, and we did nothing more than kiss, and the relationship ended when we moved a few months later. However, I cannot imagine doing such a thing with my daughters. All I can think is that Mum was vicariously enjoying a few outings, given my father's constant absences. But the long-term impact of this situation was that I had the notion that I should gratefully accept any man's interest in me. It's taken me almost a lifetime to understand that about myself, and I'm sure my mother didn't intend that at all.

At university, I wanted the respect and attention of boys, but I had no idea how to get it in a way I could manage. It was still common then to have men whistle at women and for men to think they had a right to say and do what they liked. At eighteen, I remember walking with a smaller young woman into the communal dining room in the halls of residence, where I had only arrived a couple of weeks before. A male third-year medical student stood up and yelled out at the top of his voice to the gang of boys with whom he was seated, 'Look at these two – one tall and one short but both with the same-sized tits!' The whole dining hall stared. It was utterly humiliating, but not uncommon, as I soon learnt.

My genuine naivete sometimes had me ending up in the situations any parents would hope their daughters could avoid. At eighteen and not long after returning to Australia, I walked about nine kilometres alone in the dark at two a.m. (wearing only a long black nightdress masquerading as an evening gown – all I could afford) after a Monash University ball. Over the course of the evening, the perfectly-nice-when-sober chemistry tutor who had invited me had turned into a drunken maniac. He now wanted sex in his car as reimbursement for the ticket, before kicking on with the boys elsewhere. I said I'd thought it was a date and that when he had invited me he was offering to pay for my ticket. Fine, he said, get out of the car, and he drove off, leaving me in a totally unfamiliar part of Melbourne which had a less than salubrious reputation. I had nothing to cover my dress and no money. I took off my high heels and walked along the main roads. I wasn't even sure where to go; I was freezing cold and I was too frightened to ask anyone for directions. It's probably hard to imagine now how scary it was, given we have mobile phones and bus stops with maps. Every time a car came past me, I would step into the shadows to hide. I spent the next day in bed nursing my sore feet and feeling stupid and sorry for myself. The day after, I went to the chemistry department and requested a change of tutor. Even at the time, there would have been other young women who would have called out this behaviour, but typically I blamed myself.

I did have some wonderful friendships with young men at university, but they were going through their own journey of self-discovery and trying to work out how to come out and proud about their sexual preferences. But despite the stresses of their own lives, they were fun and made me feel safe.

I see now that my inexperience with interacting with the opposite sex compounded the subliminal messages which were common at the time. Those messages suggested that to be attractive to men, women needed to be capable and clever, but not too clever. While women's rights were beginning to become more prominent in the 1970s, change was slow. For example, the principle of equal pay for equal work was introduced in 1969, but this wasn't adopted by the Public Service until 1973. It was 1978 before a woman even first read the national news on the ABC.

In laboratory-based classes in first and second year university, where we worked in small groups of three or four, I always automatically offered to take the notes and stepped back to let the boys do the hands-on components. In one physiology practical, where we operated on mice to remove their ovaries for an experiment, I recall observing the three boys in my group doing the surgery shoddily, but I was not brave enough to suggest that they go more slowly and carefully. We had been warned that mice might eat each other if there was an open wound. When the boys had run off to footy practice, I topped up the anaesthetic and restitched the mouse's abdominal wound. (It survived.)

Many of the pressures on young women in the early 1970s resulted from the fact that it was a time of social transformation in Australia. Women's liberation and gay liberation were part of the new permissive society which also offered universal healthcare and free tertiary education. The Mother's Benefit was introduced to support single mothers; before then, babies resulting from unplanned pregnancies were often relinquished unwillingly for adoption.

Women had never had so much choice, but some of us still didn't know what to choose. Women began to use the term 'Ms' instead of Miss or Mrs. I can remember being harangued by some academic friends of Peter's because I had chosen to change my name when I got married. He had wanted me to keep my maiden name, but my name was shared by someone else who also lived in Melbourne. I also liked Peter's surname better than mine, so I stuck to my guns and changed my name to his.

Women's increasing independence was not recognised by everyone. When Peter and I wanted to secure a loan to buy a house and Peter was always too busy to go to the bank, I went to see the bank manager. He was pleasant enough, but he told me to send my husband in to discuss business with him. I was furious, but did not even know how to respond.

In the end, my father organised the bank loan for us. My father was unfailingly courteous, and kind both to and about everyone. He was totally reliable, and never once can I recall him saying he would do something without following through. Growing up, I thought all men were like him. So, if I was ever let down by a man, I found a million excuses for him rather than to admit he was unreliable. I just thought that men everywhere were there to be counted on.

My father always made me feel safe, and even though I love the notion of taking risks, I like to feel that someone else has my safety as one of their priorities. I never quite got over the men's lack of concern of potential danger that was present on the Patagonian trip. Perhaps it is also genetic – if you (figuratively, as a prehistoric man) are busy hunting a woolly mammoth, you need to focus entirely on it and not be sidetracked by an open wound on your foot. Maybe these men were all risk-insensitive, while I was risk-aware. Peter certainly continues to push the boundaries well into his seventies, and even though he is not my responsibility, I worry for him. But I have finally learnt that I cannot be responsible for everyone else's health and safety all the time, that men can look after themselves, and the only person who should be responsible for my safety is me.

Looking back now, I can see that my character trait of trying to please has been a defining characteristic in my life. What began, perhaps, as trying to fit in with others as I moved school sometimes resulted in my being too agreeable. I was aware, on the Patagonian trip, that I rarely shared my fears or misgivings with others, and tried to find the best in everyone and every situation. While that may be seen as a good thing, the downside is that I am, as mentioned earlier, far too forgiving. My optimism that I can make things work out once led a former boss to call me, in my fifties, a Pollyanna, which I note is described in the dictionary as 'a person characterised by irrepressible optimism and a tendency to find good in everything'. The truth is that, whatever happens, my default position is to see it through a rose-coloured lens. Once I let any doubts in, I lie awake at night and worry rather than share those doubts with others.

The imperative to fit in clouded my sight for much of my life. I feel it took me a very long time to understand what I wanted in my life as opposed to what was wanted by those around me, whether this be workmates, friends or family.

As the children got older, I began to work a little bit more, until eventually, when they were all in secondary school, I worked full-time. I worked hard. By that time, Peter and I had separated, and I wanted to be sure I was offered employment every year, so I rarely said no to any chance to earn extra money. I always was home when the children were home from school but that meant I often was catching up or preparing for meetings late at night when they slept. Years flashed by in a blur of fatigue, a situation which I know to be common for many women working in academia.

There were many times when I felt torn between my work and my children, but I have never once regretted putting my children first. But also like those who have delayed or taken significant time out of their career to raise a family, I lived with constant anxiety that I might not be reappointed each year. This fear was compounded by the fact that I chose not to travel overseas to conferences because I did not want to leave the children. International collaboration is one of the markers of success for an academic, and while it is easy now via the internet, it was not always the case.

I did not get permanent employment or tenure until I was well into my fifties and an associate professor. For so much of my career, when I was rushing off to collect kids from school or take them to sports training, chess competitions or the myriad activities which alter the start and end time of school, I felt like I was flying by the seat of my pants. I often felt like an academic imposter, despite the fact that I was achieving many of the key performance indicators set down by the universities in which I worked. And then finally, in 2015, after years of hard work of writing and occasionally winning grant applications, and publishing papers and books, I was promoted to professor.

I observed a real shift in myself. I suddenly realised that sometimes I could say 'no' to work or offers of collaboration that were outside my area of interest. And instead of worrying about whether I would ever live up to expectations of academia, I began to believe before I delivered a talk, that people would want to hear what I had to say. I finally believed that I am worthy of my title. I know many academic women who feel this way, but I have never heard a man express it. Maybe they feel this way, but just don't share it.

Reality check 2020

Over the last thirty-five years, the Patagonian trip provided a kind of reality check in my life. Although I rarely articulated it, I would sometimes judge the quality of a current experience against a similar one on the trip. When I was tired, wet, cold, exhausted or starving, I would sometimes think, 'Is it as hard as Patagonia?' When I saw a view of incredible beauty either close or distant, I might think, 'But is it as beautiful as in Patagonia?' For so long I have rated Patagonia as a turning point in my life that I had not even considered the impact of many other events, real or imagined, in the making of me.

When I first decided to write the diaries in 1985, it was because I wanted to play a meaningful part in the field trip. I knew that I was (and still am) a good observer, and that I record information accurately. Knowing I would be travelling with others with experience in fieldwork, I imagined it might the only contribution I could make.

Of course, I can see that my contribution was much greater than that. I really was a member of the team and I worked hard. I am sure, despite my ups and downs, that I was valued by the other team members. I still feel pleased to have been part of an expedition that contributed to some new discoveries.

So if I could find them, would the diaries add any more to the record of the science of that field trip? Documentaries on the natural world are now common, and time-lapse photography, telephoto lenses, and webcams allow TV and media viewers access to detail of animal life once never imagined. But much less is shown about the challenges faced by researchers trying to understand the natural world. I wanted to write some of that, so that people understand that getting thirty seconds of good footage of an animal eating may have required weeks of fieldwork. But I also know there were other kinds of interesting information in my diaries. For example, I had recorded details of plants and trees wherever we were camped, as well as details of Indian herbal remedies for illness. I have not been able to reproduce them. And now I can't recall what else might have been in there.

When I began writing this account almost five years, ago, it was at a time of my life when I had experienced some momentous changes. I had willingly spent a large proportion of my life looking after others, at the expense of looking after myself. My father had just died, my siblings and I had emptied and sold our family home, and my own children were forging their adult lives. I suddenly felt a little lost without the anchors that had kept me calm in times of trouble. Whenever I had a sleepless night, I would often dwell on the fate that had befallen the diaries and bones, and wonder whether if I had the diaries I would understand the twists and turns my life had taken. It seemed natural to look to the past to see how much the trip of 1985–86 had contributed to the me of today.

Now that I have had the chance to concentrate on my memories and sift through details from my past, I realise that the makings of the Patagonian explorer were there from childhood, in my fascination for other cultures, my interest in the natural world and my desire for adventure. With the exception of the year in Johannesburg, most of my previous adventures had been in my imagination. I now see myself as a young woman who had a million dreams, some of which were dashed by her interrupted education and insecurities. But the same elements forged the tenacity needed for some different dreams.

The diaries of Patagonia represented much more than the record of our journey. It was my first ever sustained effort at writing. At a time when I recognised that I neither wanted to be a child psychologist nor a dance therapist, I had hoped that my writing of the diaries about my husband's important work would achieve two things. I wanted to record his work in a format that I perceived was worthy of his academic standing and, I suspect, I wanted to prove myself worthy of him. Small wonder then, that in subsequent years I could bring myself to tears thinking about the details of our trip that were lost in the diaries. But perhaps it was because I also recognised that something much bigger – my naïve and idealistic views of myself, of my relationship, and of the world – had been lost as well.

The many stories in my primary school composition books, as would be expected of a girl who loved Enid Blyton books, describe the girl protagonists as adventurers: curious, brave and ultimately overcoming hardships to succeed in their quest. As a child, I was thrilled about the idea of being a pioneer woman. I wanted to be the capable one who saved the day.

Patagonia showed me that real adventure comes at a cost. Hard physical work, a poor diet, extremes of temperature, deaths of animals, being constantly unwashed, always speaking in a different language, and being the only woman, all made it hard. I was happy to share all of those difficulties to be experiencing it with Peter.

But I recognise now that despite being in his company constantly, I was lonely for my husband. And when we finished the trip, he had his field notes and tissue samples to continue his work. While I had many memories, I had nothing tangible to show for the trip, apart from an understanding that providing field assistance was not the way to get closer to my husband.

In many ways, my life has been characterised by the loss which is inevitable when one moves frequently. As I left each school, and each state or country, I said goodbye to my often only recently made friends. Sometimes, I also said goodbye to my family. In those days, letters were the usual form of communication, as long-distance telephone calls were only for adults. Sometimes, I would write to a school friend, but the reality was that our paths would be unlikely to cross again, and the letters would become less frequent and then cease as our lives grew apart. It seems that over and over I have lost the witnesses to important parts of my life.

I still have many of the letters my parents and siblings wrote to me at boarding school, and that now long-lost university friends wrote to me in university breaks. I also have some letters from past boyfriends, and from two people who have remained friends for over forty years. I can see my obsession with hoarding them shows a need for some kind of corroboration for my life, to remind me that yes, I was there. As I once read in someone else's memoir, 'Being left with a wobbly memory is another state of loneliness.'

I would still like to see the diaries again. The feeling now, though, is one of mild curiosity, like one has for an old not-so-close friend one hasn't seen for many years.

Thinking about how to hunt for the diaries has allowed me to find so much of my past which I had forgotten, and I actually feel pretty good about what I have found. I overcame my early academic failures in totally unexpected ways. I have had the interesting life for which I yearned. I have three amazing children, and my contribution to their lives is my greatest achievement. I lost the diaries, but in my search to re-create them, I found myself.

Patagonia was a great adventure, but my life so far has been a much greater one.

For those interested in the fieldwork

Kangaroos, koalas and possums have so long been used as part of Australian tourism campaigns that few people realise that there are about eighty-five species of American marsupials, belonging to four families. (Families are large groups in zoological terms —the cat family for example, includes both domestic cats and lions.) Given that fossil evidence of American marsupials is older than any in Australia, naturalists have long been curious about whether the American marsupials entered Australia through the Gondwana land-bridge and then radiated out and diversified into the amazing array of marsupials we now have.

One argument against American marsupials being the progenitor of all Australian marsupials was found in the behaviour of their sperm. In all the American marsupials examined before the 1980s, sperm travelled in pairs, head stuck to head. In contrast, the sperm of all Australian marsupials, including possums and kangaroos and koalas, travelled singly, as they do in humans.

A forty-million-year-old skull, identical to the modern day *monito* skull, suggested this little animal (*Dromiciops gliroides*) may not have changed over millions of years. An important aim of the Patagonian trip was to collect sperm from the marsupial possum. If the sperm travelled singly, it would suggest the family to which *monitos* belong as being a likely progenitor of the Australian marsupials, given that males in the other three families of American marsupials all produce the unusual paired sperm.

While we did not successfully trap any *monitos* in 1985, we had managed to purchase over twenty from the locals, and we subsequently kept some of them for several weeks (the travelling *monitos*) to monitor their reproductive development. Ultimately, one male, Maurico, had provided semen that showed all the signs of his sperm being solo travellers. But he wasn't completely mature, and December in 1985 did not match our expectations for the usual breeding season. Of course, Mauricio was one animal only, and caution limited the conclusion which could be drawn from this study.

The second aim of the 1985 trip was to try to find living specimens of the most southerly distributed American marsupial, the Patagonian opossum, *Lestodelphys halli*. The last time living specimens had been captured was in 1935 in Argentine Patagonia. The many little jawbones we had so laboriously dissected from owl pellets were what had been stolen alongside my diaries in London.

The third aim of the trip was to collect sperm from the *yaca* (*Thylamys elegans*), a small carnivorous mouse-like marsupial found in Chile. Despite a solid week of trapping, we had trapped many adult females plus juvenile males and females, but no adult males in breeding condition.

While they were the three main purposes of the trip, as for any scientific expedition, an enormous amount of additional information was collected which was distributed to scientists for other purposes.

In the pile of information Peter had now shared with me, I was interested, for example, to find a 'Preliminary Report' dated 29 October 1985, handwritten by me, presumably under Peter's instruction. It was written to the *Jefe*, or boss, of the Parque Nacional at Puyehue. It described the exact locations of the traplines, the dates of trapping (20–29 October 1985) and a description and measurements of the forty mice which were caught. Obviously, we were not trying to catch the mice; they simply went into the traps in which we were hoping to catch *monitos*. But they still provided information which was valuable for someone.

I was amused to see that of thirty-two male mice, sixteen were subsequently recaptured on the following nights. Half were recaptured once only but some were recaptured three or four times. In comparison, only six female mice were captured, four once and two twice. It's true that overall there were more male mice caught, but it did seem the male mice either did not learn as fast or were prepared to take greater risks than the females. In the report, it stated that 'since the males are preparing for the breeding season, as judged by testicular size, this high male recapture rate may reflect searching activity or territorial aggressive components of male behaviour associated with the breeding season'. The report also observed that while the vaginae in female olive field mice were not patent (that is, not ready for breeding), in the long-tailed rice rat, the females all had discernable vaginal openings, and the males had 'large palpable scrotal testes'. I find it fascinating the way biology and behaviour are so related.

In 2018, Peter went to Chile. He had recently started doing some work with a Chilean vet who had come to Australia to undertake a PhD on marsupials. She had told him of the Senda Darwin Biological Station on Chiloe Island. Senda Darwin had, in the last decade, set up nesting boxes for *monito* research, as well as a series of radial traplines for regular monitoring of the health, behaviour and reproductive status of these animals.

Peter and his colleagues visited Chiloe to try to get some data on the *monitos'* sperm. In the 1985 trip, Mauricio's sperm had suggested that *monito* sperm travelled solo, but more examples were needed from males in natural breeding condition to confirm it.

In the trip north to Pichidangi, which took place in January, 1986, we successfully trapped lots of adult female *yacas* and many immature females and males, but no large males. Peter had revisited the site in September 1991 after doing some work for the World Health Organisation in Peru. However, on that occasion he only caught one female. The weather was very cold, and he surmised that maybe most of the animals were hibernating. So he still had yet to successfully examine the sperm of male *yacas* in peak breeding season. The 1991 trip suggested September was too early to catch males in the breeding season, and the 1986 trip suggested January was too late, so he had high hopes of catching a reproductively active male if he trapped animals in

November 2019, an idea supported by the local Chilean researchers working with him.

In the end, due to the large number of holiday houses which had been built, they were unable to find the exact spot where we had trapped forty years before. They set up camp at a nearby pristine area at Puquen.

A week or so later, Peter jubilantly announced that they had trapped many *yacas* – seven large adult males and twenty-nine adult females. Three tiny babies which had also been trapped looked to be on a growth trajectory which would make them a similar size to the young animals we caught in January 1986. Most exciting was the news that males seemed to be at the peak of reproduction, as they were producing paired sperm. Also of enormous interest was that some of the males had lost a significant amount of fur, suggesting their physical condition was deteriorating.

The reason this is so interesting is that it is similar to Australia's marsupial mouse, antechinus, where the males, like the males of several small to medium carnivorous marsupials, are known to die after a single breeding season. In antechinus, the females only ovulate after they have mated and all the males have died from the stress of mating activities. Females have special storage areas in their oviducts which allow them to store the sperm of several different males.

Males only undergo a single cycle of spermatogenesis to produce fertile sperm for the mating season. Females mate multiple times with different males and produce a litter of eight to ten offspring with as many as five different fathers. Once the male has mated, it dies, allowing the females and babies less competition for the local food supplies. A few weeks after the breeding season is over, not a single male remains alive in the forest. It is fascinating to think that these Chilean *yacas* appear to show a similar post-breeding season die-off to some of our small Australian carnivorous marsupials. Another field trip will be needed to confirm it.

Our discovery of the rare Patagonian opossum bones in Patagonia in 1985, which had represented many, many days of climbing up cliffs, collecting and dissecting owl pellets, was superseded soon after by zoologist Oliver Pearson from University of California Berkeley.

Given his lifelong commitment and annual visits to Patagonia for many years, it was wonderful that he should find, within a year of our search, two live specimens. Both were trapped almost a thousand kilometres north of where we had collected owl pellets. Since then, other live specimens have been caught and their captive behaviour recorded in detail (Martin et al. 2011). Despite this, I am sure that if the 'bones' we so painstakingly collected and which were subsequently stolen were ever recovered, the British Museum would still be happy to have them, given this little opossum is still considered to be rare.

References

Birney, E.C., Monjeau, J.A., Phillips, C.J., Sikes, R.S., Kim, I., '*Lestodelphys halli*: new information on a poorly known Argentine marsupial', *Mastozoología Neotropical*, 1996, 3(2):171–181.

Frankham, G., Temple-Smith, P., 'Absence of mammary development in male Monitos gliroides: another link to the Australian marsupial fauna', *Journal of Mammalogy*, 2012, 93(2): 572–578.

Grant T.R., Temple-Smith, P.D., 'Observations on torpor in the small marsupial Monitos australis (Marsupialia: Microbiotheriidae) from southern Chile', pp. 273–277 in *Possums and Possums: Studies in Evolution* (Archer M., ed.), 1987, Surrey Beatty and Royal Zoological Society of New South Wales, Sydney.

Larrain, H. 'Por los caminos de America: En pos de Luis Pena Guzman'. *Eco-Antropologia*, 23 February 2008.

Martin G.M., Udrizar-Sauthier, D.E., 'Observations on the captive behavior of the rare Patagonian opossum Lestodelphys halli (Thomas, 1921) (Marsupialia, Didelphimorphia, Didelphidae)', *Mammalia* 75 (2011): 281–286.

Simpson, G.G., 1972. *Didelphidae from the Chapaldmalal Formation in the Museo Municipal de Ciencias Naturales de Mar del Plata*, Publicaciones del Museo Municipal de Ciencias Naturales 'Lorenzo Scaglia', 2:1–29.

Spangler, P. J. and Staines, C. L., 'Luchoelmis, a new genus of Elmidae (Coleoptera) from Chile and Argentina' (2002), *Insecta Mundi*, 555. http://digitalcommons.unl.edu/insectamundi/555

Temple-Smith, P.D., 'Sperm structure and marsupial phylogeny', pp. 171–194 in *Possums and Possums: Studies in Evolution* (Archer M., ed.), 1987, Surrey Beatty and Royal Zoological Society of New South Wales, Sydney.

Thomas, O., 1921, 'A new genus of opossum from southern Patagonia', *Annals and Magazine of Natural History*, Series 9, 8:136–139.

—, 1929, 'The Mammals of Señor Budin's Patagonian expedition,

1927–28', *Annals and Magazine of Natural History*, Series 10, 4:35–45.

Wilson, D.E. and Mittermeier, R.A. (eds), *The Handbook of the Mammals of the World 2015. Vol. 5 Monotremes and Marsupials*. Lynx Edicions.

From *Woman's Day* article, February 1986, page 43:

The possibility that a South American marsupial could be an ancestor of the Australian marsupial is to be explored by Peter Temple-Smith, a reproductive biologist and lecturer in anatomy in Melbourne's Monash University. Peter will try to establish the link by examining the sperm of a marsupial the natives call Monito del Monte, on a trip to South America with his wife, Meredith, who is a research psychologist, plus one of his MA students. They will be guided by a South American entomologist and his assistant. "If Peter finds what he is looking for it could prove the old theory that South America was joined to Antarctica and Antarctica was joined to Australia" said Meredith. In a land where women are kept in the background, Meredith, who has been learning Spanish, will dress like a man and cover her blond hair with a scarf. She will also undertake her own project, studying animal behaviour.

Acknowledgements

Many people offered advice and support along my writing journey. Long-standing supporters Priscilla Pyett and Anne Mitchell offered honest and regular critique which moved my manuscript from a simple record of the field trip to something far more meaningful. I am grateful for our friendship of forty-plus years. Longtime friends Tom and Gina Grant, as always, offered thoughtful commentary, and Tom's memories of his earlier trapping trip in Patagonia with Peter prompted some recall of details.

Thanks to those who provided encouragement after reading various drafts: my niece Romany Rzechowicz, Ron Slamowicz, my son-in-law Matthew Nolan, Meg Mappin, Michael Liley, Gemma Bilardi and Marie Pirotta.

I would like to thank Checho and Pedro for being my Patagonian family during our journey, and watching out for me during our travels. Without them and Lucho, there would have been no journey to record! And finally my deepest thanks to Peter Temple-Smith, for introducing me to the world of native animals. He pushed me to the limit in Patagonia, but I have never regretted a moment!

www.ingramcontent.com/pod-product-compliance
Lightning Source LLC
Chambersburg PA
CBHW071436080526
44587CB00014B/1867